Radical Principals

Radical Principals is a guidebook for K-12 leaders looking for creative ways, beyond the status quo, to support and nurture school communities in the wake of unprecedented obstacles. In-service principals understandably rely on existing protocols and district policies to solve day-to-day problems, but do you ever wonder whether these quick fixes are preventing you from making a more lasting, transformative change? Radical Principals are those school leaders who recognize that every child, especially disadvantaged ones living through inequities, need adults lighting their path with inventive and evidence-based opportunities for success.

This inspirational yet pragmatic book provides novel strategies and solutions for balancing common concerns—curriculum, school safety, high-stakes testing, parental concerns, among others—while advancing your long-term vision for your school. These audacious, yet controlled approaches will help you maneuver around both the stubborn obstacles facing children in the greatest need of supports and your own blind spots and unintended biases. Spanning bureaucratic roadblocks, systemic injustice, communication breakdowns, and more, each chapter is rich with scenario-based challenges and leadership practices that don't merely resolve the issues at hand but further help you advance your school toward a holistically equitable and supportive climate.

Michael S. Gaskell is Principal of Hammarskjold Middle School in East Brunswick, New Jersey, USA, and the author of *Leading Schools Through Trauma: A Data-Driven Approach to Helping Children Heal*.

Other Eye On Education Books Available from Routledge

(www.routledge.com/eyeoneducation)

Radical Principals

A Blueprint for Long-Term Equity and Stability at School

Michael S. Gaskell

Routledge
Taylor & Francis Group

NEW YORK AND LONDON

Cover image: ©Shutterstock

First published 2023
by Routledge
605 Third Avenue, New York, NY 10158

and by Routledge
4 Park Square, Milton Park, Abingdon, Oxon, OX14 4RN

Routledge is an imprint of the Taylor & Francis Group, an informa business

Library of Congress Cataloging-in-Publication Data
Names: Gaskell, Michael S., 1970- author.
Title: Radical principals: a blueprint for long-term equity and stability at
school / Michael S. Gaskell.
Description: New York, NY: Routledge, 2023. | Includes bibliographical
references. | Identifiers: LCCN 2022026182 (print) | LCCN 2022026183
(ebook) | ISBN 9781032231082 (hardback) | ISBN 9781032229287
(paperback) | ISBN 9781003275718 (ebook)
Subjects: LCSH: School principals--United States. | School management
and organization--United States. | School environment--United States.
| Educational leadership--United States.
Classification: LCC LB2831.92.G37 2023 (print) | LCC LB2831.92 (ebook)
| DDC 371.2/0120973—dc23/eng/20220713
LC record available at https://lccn.loc.gov/2022026182
LC ebook record available at https://lccn.loc.gov/2022026183

ISBN: 978-1-032-23108-2 (hbk)
ISBN: 978-1-032-22928-7 (pbk)
ISBN: 978-1-003-27571-8 (ebk)

DOI: 10.4324/9781003275718

Typeset in Palatino
by SPi Technologies India Pvt Ltd (Straive)

Contents

Preface

When you walk into any school, you can immediately sense the climate of the classrooms, halls, offices, and gymnasiums. It's as if you possess a sixth sense to know intuitively what is behind the door. This is not just what is visible, although what is seen matters. Friendly, welcoming posters and a prideful appearance that make clear the values of a school certainly help set or, more likely, reinforce the underlying tone in certain schools. In others, the dark, dismal setting is a negatively reinforcing environment, sadly led by those who are primarily responsible for the dim school atmosphere.

I have had the fortune of being in hundreds of schools over the course of a quarter of a century in my professional capacity. I have observed an overpowering presence of equity and nurture in some, and a cold, unwelcoming environment in others. Mostly, I have witnessed those in between, with some positive elements, and other with areas that need development. The majority of schools, their leaders and faculty set out to work every day because they cared deeply enough about children that they wanted to make a difference in their lives. That is an awesome place to grow from.

Schools that separate themselves, those that distinguish remarkable character, do not happen accidentally. They are forged through hard work, creativity, and promise. They are guided by leaders with the courage to oppose injustices, even those that could be detrimental to their own professional aspirations. They know that, above all, equity and a thriving learning community are paramount to long term success for all children.

These distinctive signs have emerged in the hundreds of schools I have visited and observed. While these are anecdotal experiences, noticeable patterns have materialized. In fear-based organizations, leaders are either inconsistent or egotistical, or both. There is no continuity, no clear messaging system about a broader vision and no purpose for supporting all children.

Leaders in these organizations are simply moving through their day in triage from one reactionary moment to the next. Everything seems urgent because it is. Students are directly influenced by this distressing climate. It is no wonder that more extreme student behaviors flare up with children, and adults respond in a mirroring fashion within these negatively reinforcing school communities.

Most schools exist somewhere between a toxic, hostile environment, and those that thrive, which somehow overcome the odds and predictions that demographic statistics cannot make allowances for. Having witnessed dozens of schools that excel and seeing the value of leaders who are not only strong but courageously so, I knew that more schools could become exceptional. Therefore, we must promote the ideals that make it possible. In the context of weaving practical storylines and research together, I was compelled to share these practices, ideologies, and instructions, in this text.

I hope that, like me, you will be inspired by the solutions harvested from my work, both circumstantial and evidence-based. Combined, this approach has taught me to be a learner, as much as a teacher and to use this knowledge to create prosperous, nourishing learning communities, led from the top, but democratically fostered.

These environments are balanced, with a refreshing abundance of confident leadership, and an openness toward groundbreaking practices. Join me on this journey and start your own radical success story today.

Meet the Author

Michael S. Gaskell is Principal of Hammarskjold Middle School in East Brunswick, New Jersey, USA, and was formerly a special educator and assistant principal in Paramus, NJ. He has a podcast called Big Ideas in Small Windows and continues to model the pursuit of lifelong learning as a mentor to new principals through the New Jersey Leaders to Leaders program and regularly presents on topics relevant to today's educators. The author of *Leading Schools Through Trauma: A Data-Driven Approach to Helping Children Heal* (Routledge/Eye On Education, 2021) and *Microstrategy Magic: Confronting Classroom Challenges While Saving Time and Energy* (Rowman & Littlefield, 2020), Dr. Gaskell has published over thirty articles in *eSchoolNews, Middleweb, NASSP, ASCD Smartbrief, Edtech Smartbrief, ASCD Blog* and *Education Dive*, and has made the most-read section of ASCD Smartbrief on multiple occasions. Gaskell represented his passion about equity on The BAM radio podcast with Larry Ferlazzo in the summer of 2022.

1

Why Be Radical?

Before jumping into how to be radical, school leaders must understand why they should be, and how the decision-making process with radical approaches helps children achieve far greater outcomes than traditionally instituted practices. After all, being radical in schools brings the kind of risks most *good-enough* school leaders would understandably fear as being too dangerous, choosing instead to play it safe.

The bold nature of being radical may also appear to bring about an overwhelming workload for an educator to undertake. It feels like being radical comes with a cost. It does. Yet the cost of not being radical, of not doing anything beyond convention is far greater. Being radical does not mean being reckless. Doing so in a calculated way can produce far-reaching, rewarding outcomes for students.

If you search the meaning of the word radical, two types of definitions typically surface

◆ a math concept about *radical numbers and equations* and
◆ being *radical* in the context of social and political extremes.

DOI: 10.4324/9781003275718-1

Yet our definition of radical means thinking outside the box, of being innovative and of making drastic change in ways that are courageous. It is often nudging strategically and boldly beyond the status quo.

Radical approaches are the sorts that are crazy the day before they are brilliant. The payoff is enormous, especially for children who are disadvantaged. Students are the real winners of fearlessly Radical Principals, who vigorously and willfully demand equitable opportunities within their school community, for all. Every child, every underdog must be represented, and provided real opportunities to flourish.

What is presented in this text is not a single silver bullet. That which separates the ideology of radical leadership is the courage and perseverance to navigate through the imminent, stubborn and mundane hurdles that exist when principals aspire to develop strong school communities, ones that help all children succeed. Throughout, you will learn about principals in real scenarios, who lead the charge, often with brevity, at other times with the willfulness to maneuver cleverly around political obstacles.

These principals all keep a trained eye on helping change systems that have existed far too long, beyond practical relevance. These are outdated institutional practices that stubbornly persist due to established community norms. All students matter. Disadvantaged students, average learners, those who excel, and those who have faced unfair inequities. Radical Principals establish this value as their basis for decision-making, and approach with resolute purpose the application of long-term changes that fruitfully sustain for their students.

Disrupting the causes of barriers that endure unjustly for children provides alternate solutions for them to excel, in truly egalitarian school environments. This may not seem like a radical concept. After all, aren't we always talking about equity and learning ways to create contexts for children and families to experience the kind of equality democracy demands?

Yet, if we dig into the underbelly of subtle, powerful institutional obstacles that persist across school systems, in the trenches of classrooms, the expensive chairs of school board meeting rooms, and the larger cultural contexts surrounding school communities, we expose deep-seated barriers. Like picking up a rock and discovering a network of life crawling underneath and out of sight, these are hard to see, obscure challenges, and they must be confronted with the kind of courage that exposes them, so true change can be fostered.

To illustrate this point, let us explore a scenario that will serve as a foundation for the rest of this text. The example presented is interconnected to the many values throughout and will serve to provide scrutiny across the various challenges Radical Principals navigate through. This storyline illustrates how one principal overcame the stumbling blocks along his journey that existed beyond relevance, and how ideas like this can offer a replicable path for those interested in achieving the same kind of balanced justice within communities for all. The kind of resilience he exemplified serves as a template in institutionalizing equity that endures amidst the injustices that all too commonly block fairness for everyone.

How One Small Shy Child Changed a School's Dress Code

So often, when children attempt to advocate for a cause they believe in, adults become defensive and worse, stand by the mantra that "This is the way things have always been, so they must remain as they are," without ever examining *why* they are the way they are, or what relevance the current context has for such a contested practice.

One spring, as the weather warmed in an American northeastern town like so many, the administration reminded students about the school's dress code. They rolled out the annual announcement, and referred to the school's code of conduct. This year did not bring the usual murmurs and griping about fairness often lingering in middle-school hallways and on social media. Something far more prevailing was about to happen.

The principal was notified that a child unknown to him, other than the timid smile she would flash him in the hall as he greeted her and other students each morning had stood before the Board of Education at a public and televised meeting, advocating for a more fair and equitable dress code in the school, one that she challenged was gender-biased. Armed with a petition signed by hundreds of students, she came prepared with examples, characterizing excerpts from the dress code.

When the principal learned about this, he felt a defensive instinct to react before pushing this impulse aside. He decided instead to ask *why*, and to seek his answer by revisiting the school's dress code himself. As he looked over the dress code from a new lens, he recognized with embarrassment that there was wording contained in it that was undoubtedly gender-specific and directed specifically at female students. How could he have missed this?

The dress code had been minimally changed over the years. Until this moment, it was one of those circumstances when radical opportunities are bestowed on a leader to act. A stagnant dress code went unnoticed until it was long overdue. It was no wonder they were petitioning; the dress code was not gender-neutral, nor was it equitable.

The principal began to research the issues underlying gender bias in dress codes, the media coverage of the historic #MeToo movement and other rights groups standing up for female, and, more specifically, gender-equitable rights. He was intrigued, not only by the degree of press coverage, but also by movements among pioneering school districts in faraway communities from his East Coast school, like in Oregon and California.

The one that caught his eye was "Oregon NOW." Female students had petitioned in a well-conceived and passionate testimony to their Board of Education, lobbying for gender neutrality in their school's dress code. This made such an impression within the community that district leaders subsequently worked with the administration, staff, and families to revise the dress code. Additionally, they committed to educating staff, parents, and students about it.

The student's presentation (*Oregon Student Dress Codes*, 2016) established common phrases like, "I am not a distraction," referring to the minimization and objectification many felt when they were called out for their dress. The principal was baffled as he examined his own school's dated dress code. Confirming that it was *not* gender-neutral, and an artifact of a code of conduct that had been reprinted for years, it was inevitable that this issue moved beyond the common "it's not fair" argument to one of impassioned substance and heart.

His school's dress code was problematic in presentation for several reasons. First, it listed disciplinary action before guidelines. This signaled a negative undertone that the dress code was punitive, rather than acting as a constructive learning opportunity. Compliance was the expectation. Agreement can go so far, but most effective and motivating educators are those that do not force students to comply. Rather, they empower students to be part of a constructive path in decision making to make their school a better, more learner friendly place.

Helping students to understand that there is value in a cause, especially one that is larger than themselves is in itself an incredible learning opportunity. It is a significant experience in how learners present and commit to take part in addressing values within their community. This calls for a greater purpose, one toward more fair treatment of something so common as enforcement of a school's dress code.

Like many of the institutionalized methods for communicating inequity to members of a school community, the dress code was written to suggest that it required obedience. This approach provoked rebellion. It was only a matter of time and broader initiatives like #MeToo that motivated a push against compliance, especially when the established norm was outdated. As this principal recalled, there is more power in persuasion than push. Force only gets you so far. Enlisting participation encourages collaboration and consensus.

The first two items outlined in the dress code were undoubtedly scripted for female students, conveying that expectations were disproportionately focused on them. Secondary dress code expectations followed, and were measured in broader terms. This language was directed at one gender, never mind a second or a third. Here was the general idea stated, standing as items 1 and 2:

◆ *Clothing must cover the front and the back of the student (off-the-shoulder tops, tops with spaghetti straps, bare midriffs, halter tops, and tank tops are not permitted).*

◆ *Shorts or skirts must not be too short or too tight fitting.*

Schools and districts who effectively regulate student dress maintain that a dress code is necessary, but they balance this with fair and sensible agreement, consistent with community standards. Dress code is something students can and will see value in and take part of. Calling for safety, non-offensive wording, and gender-neutral descriptions of length, size, etc., are the qualifications for a value-based, gender-neutral dress code in most communities.

The school's dress code was revised, as the leadership committed to removing any gender-specific content as well as by promoting a fair and equitable set of guidelines. Individuals from the school community were advised, and participated in the revisions. Today, the new dress code starts along these lines:

Our School encourages all students to be able to dress comfortably for school without fear of or disruption to their learning process.

This introduction establishes that questions about dress code would not be at the cost of disrupting student learning as a key tenant in a fair and equitable dress code. Dress code should not be on par with significantly more severe disciplinary matters like fighting, illegal substances, threats, or other significant infractions. Additionally, there is a common understanding applied that certain body parts must be covered for *all* students, and that is determined within the values of the given community. These values change over time.

A contemporary dress code prioritizes safety, addresses offensive language, and exposure of undergarments – all in gender-neutral language. Never again was a description specifically geared to female attire in this school, and the emphasis was on safety as well as a respectful, non-biased standard. This is something that helped redirect toward impartial treatment rather than targeting individuals because of their identity.

Dress code has been part of a broader challenge that gained national attention about gender fairness. The principal's eyes widened as a teacher, administrator, and father about what fair treatment should look like for all students. He was influenced by one small, shy child, and, thanks to children like her, his school is a better place. The dress code is constructed fairly for all students. If you are wondering about your own dress code, think about the influence you can have with some subtle, yet significant, shifts in language. As you will see, subtle and significant approaches play a large part in many radical changes for the better.

Beginner's Mindset in Radical Leadership

Principals as educational leaders often possess considerable professional knowledge. They are typically recruited for their position because of their expertise and likeness as educators. Yet Radical Principals do not limit their influence to their own expertise. That would be a costly mistake, limiting one's scope to a fixed, either/or mindset. Instead, these school leaders approach topics like school dress code with a Beginner's Mindset.

Beginner's Mindset has roots in Zen Buddhism. Being open, eager, and careful not to hold onto preconceived beliefs or expectations when studying a context or issue helps the leader to explore nontraditional solutions and alternatives. Importantly, this occurs even when studying or demonstrating mastery at an advanced level, just as a beginner would.

If the principal who was dealing with the dress code problem dismissed or minimized the student's concerns, he would have done so with a closed mindset, based solely on his own prior knowledge, assumptions and experience. Limiting beliefs inhibit the leader's ability to expand to more adaptable solutions. With closed minds and assumptions, the school becomes a place where limiting beliefs overtake opportunity and exploration is discouraged.

The school leader investigating the dress code had the courage to set aside his assumptions and as Radical Principals do, reconsidered his position on dress code. The outcome? His school became a better, fairer environment for all learners. Not just for young ladies. Everyone recognizes the benefit of sensible, fair, and equitable changes, like a dress code for all. Radical Principals seize on moments like this, willing to maintain an open mindset, the kind that enables positive change to take root. There is sustaining power in positive change.

Adam Grant (2021) explores open mindset in the context of a broad failure, from the leadership at a quickly forgotten, once incredibly successful company named Blackberry. From 2009 to 2014, Blackberry was wiped off the technology map, owning 50% of the smartphone market share to grasping just 1% in those short five years. Radical leaders are willing to change course to remain current. Blackberry's leadership did not, refusing to change their vision, and they lost big.

When we rethink our beliefs, we remain open to better, more innovative options in a fast-changing world. Radical Principals carry tremendous responsibility. They hold the academic lives of children in their hands, and that is even more profound when you consider their impact on disadvantaged and at-risk children, who are more vulnerable to their leadership influence.

Unlike Blackberry, a very different organization, Amazon transformed itself from exclusively serving as a book retailer to one-stop shopping for virtually anything from food to technology to clothing, all guaranteed to be on your doorstep in two days. Love or hate them, they had the leadership to be radical, and transform. They adapted to an economy and changes that demanded their versatile service approach.

Radical Change from the Middle

Faculty members bring a litany of concerns to school leaders, most often with the best of intentions. They often inquire with disbelief about why something is the way it is, why change cannot happen so quickly or easily, if at all or how it is possible that the principal, as the school leader, cannot resolve a plainly obvious issue. After all, if it is the right thing to do, why can't we just do it, they wonder?

On the other side of this are opposing forces from people and institutions: parents, central office, board of education members and others all with expectation that the principal manage issues, often in direct contrast to the context a faculty member may see. Institutionalized guidelines can often inhibit the ability to enact change. These hurdles include pre-existing and archaic policy, finance by-laws, or other barriers.

What those on either side of the principal cannot easily see are the challenging circumstances faced by their school leader. Principals are quite literally in between, serving in the role of *middle manager*. They often encounter forces that are opposing, or at least conflicting from either side of their role as a building leader. These are the major components of the barriers that Radical Principals must learn to work around. Depending on the school framework, some principals have more given power, and others hold less sway.

Regardless, all principals sit structurally at some variation of the intermediate point of the organizational leadership power structure, with others standing as their superiors, while faculty and staff report to them. Still other individuals in the dynamic school community represent their customer base- including school's families.

Being aware of these structural dynamics is one of the most fundamental factors in learning how to maneuver; to shape and enact radical change, and to improve a school environment. To be radical, sometimes, the principal must take chances, big and small. These include the risk of begging for forgiveness, rather than asking for permission.

Beg for Forgiveness, Rather than Ask for Permission

Radical timing is explored in depth in Chapter 3. It is worth highlighting briefly why using this strategy pays such big dividends, in relationship to being situated in middle-management positions. The example that follows illustrates how, without a radical decisiveness, a principal would have unnecessarily lost the direct support provided to children by a school counselor, possibly in times of crisis for nine full school days, out of a 180-day calendar. That is a monumental and unacceptable loss of student support time, especially for those most in need.

Delaying much-needed support services that offer students critical help is inexcusable. Less radical leaders do not always see a way around bureaucratic challenges that postpone needed support for children, and that is why there are times when precious aid, and the opportunity to assist children are lost. Students lose, and not just any. The children most in need lose out. Disadvantaged children are at greatest risk, and they cannot be lost to compliance. Remember that as you read on.

Returning to the principal fighting against nine days of lost counselor support time for children, the school was expected to follow a literal path to school law and board policy that was so harmful, it was fleecing support to at-risk students. In fact, the very intention to make the school climate better was perpetuating a harmful result that had to be addressed, as it was quite damaging to children. This served as a red alert, a signal. When students lose, a principal must step in to act, even courageously on his own. The scenario follows.

In September, 2010, a Rutgers University college student leapt to his death from the George Washington Bridge, after his roommate had "outed" him for his sexual orientation, on social media (Parker, 2012). The story is tragic and continues to serve as a baseline for a worst-case scenario of online bullying. Suicide is unquestionably the ultimate tragedy that results from behavior caused by the harmful impact of another.

New Jersey politicians responded by implementing one of the most proactive revisions to anti-bullying law in history. Previous bullying laws were moderate and these new provisions were farther-reaching in investigative practices and processes. Training occurred statewide, at school localities and a process for implementing the bullying amendment was instituted.

The intent of this revision was worthy. If we could help children find a way out of being bullied and be more preventive in aiding targeted children, while working to change an aggressor's behaviors, we could better protect and support children who needed it. What's more, addressing school culture would be an add-on bonus, as the offending children were held accountable and schoolwide programs aimed to reduce bullying behavior. The goal was to establish supportive interventions for all to learn from their experience. The opportunity to focus on the future, a better path for all was possible.

Political forces drove most of the initial implementation of this amendment, and while the theoretical intent was spot on, the practical approach or at least varying interpretations of it, were often problematic. In some schools, any time a person alleged bullying, the school was mandated to open an investigation. On the surface, this may sound sensible, even righteous but let us take a closer look at the practicality of this process, and how it can have the opposite outcome, instead causing harm.

If in every instance a child or adult accuses a person of bullying in a school context, the school must conduct a thorough two-week, process-oriented investigation, the school resources are taxed. This is the case even when evidence exists that an incident was not bullying. This process drives the investigator to focus almost exclusively on the burden of investigation protocols.

In New Jersey, a school counselor trained in bullying investigation procedures typically conducts the investigation as an impartial third party, rather than a school administrator. This means they are pulled from their counseling duties and immersed in the investigation process, including the requirement for meticulous documentation, coordination of student interviews and other potential evidence.

When this happens, the school counselor can no longer focus on direct student support, and instead must concentrate on the painstaking task of fulfilling legal requirements of the investigation process. This has the effect of removing the counselor from supports for children, at times when children are in most need of their counseling interventions. They are occupied by an investigation, which may not have any substance or legitimately justify the formal investigation that is underway.

The additional challenge with bullying investigations arises when with any allegation, it causes a negative school climate when counter claims of bullying are often and unnecessarily triggered by emotionally charged, accused parties. In most bullying allegations, it is determined that the incidents are not bullying but rather a matter of code of conduct and is a typical back-and-forth conflict between students.

This process can create an accelerant that exasperates from families, feeling compelled to defend their accused child. "Oh yea, they are making a bullying allegation against my child? I want an investigation against their child!" Now you have two potentially unnecessary investigations, instead of one.

The other problem with this procedure is that any parent or student can make an accusation against a staff member. In one school, the numerous accusations levied against faculty almost never resulted in a confirmation that bullying had in fact occurred. This is because the matter was most often determined to be a teacher redirection, or other classroom management intervention while supervising student conduct during instruction.

In accusations against students, the bullying investigation risks becoming quite literally unrelenting, even preposterous. Schools become preoccupied with the mundane process-oriented legal obligation of investigating. They are caught in a web between two archrival families, a modern-day version of the Montagues and the Capulets.

Two feuding families consumed with quarreling over each of their children causes a cycle of hostility. In these scenarios, the investigations are unnecessary, and compound the harmful effects for which the bullying law was intended to prevent. Worse, this effect does not exclusively limit to two warring families. Student conflicts and discipline affects all of those in the school community; even those uninvolved in an issue (Epperson, 2019), infecting everyone.

True efforts at resolution offer far greater outcomes when instances are not bullying and the school officials addressing these issues already know it. Long-term success, solutions for the affected students and lasting impacts on the school community are the payoff as participants learn to become problem solvers of conflict, rather than feuding, toxic accusers. Instead of escalating unnecessary tensions, school communities can teach the value of conflict resolution, and better allocate time and resources to support children in need.

Unfortunately, there are times when faculty demonstrate a loss of judgment and they must be held accountable when treating children unfairly. This does not happen often. Imagine if incidents involving faculty were confirmed as bullying. You likely would have already known about this, complaints buzzing around social media or in the community, and with just cause. Justice should and is often served in these hyper focused incidents.

Indeed, we should openly inform those we are responsible to in our communities about the worst effects of adult intimidation on a child. Often, however, allegations of this nature are triggered by resentment, or, more commonly, misunderstanding. Accountability such as a bad grade or feeling annoyed about a teacher calling out a student for misconduct can initiate an unnecessary and costly accusation.

In allegations against faculty, adults become increasingly cautious about addressing student misconduct or academic concerns. They fear that their actions will be misconstrued and result in punitive consequences, be it a disciplinary action or a stain on their reputation. This is especially distressing for educators, who became teachers to help others, not to harm them. This contradicts good intentions to support children in ways that help them grow and develop in positive, thriving school communities. These are conditions that help children develop socially and for them to learn to resolve issues at the source.

Why This Matters

Counselors are trained to support the needs of developing young minds, as children learn to navigate the ups and downs, the roller coaster ride they inevitably travel and develop along. The school counselor, restricted to fulfilling a meticulous investigation, is absent from classrooms where she teaches life skills; remains unavailable to provide crisis management to children experiencing grief, and tragedy, and to ensure student safety with those considering harm to self or others. Social emotional needs of children call for top priority and attention by their counselors.

Children benefit from receiving interventions like group therapy, learning to develop coping strategies and by being identified in need by their school counselors. This help should be readily accessible to them by affording counselors the time.

Put plainly, the urgent call to assist children in need is more valuable than investigating known non-bullying incidents. So how do we fix this problem, when most bullying allegations (75% in the previously mentioned school) are confirmed as not bullying, already known to be a matter of conflict, prior to initiating a prolonged investigation?

The Fix One School Leader Discovered

Avoidable investigations burdened the counselor and damaged school culture. The principal examined the data. Half of the accusations that were investigated were already known to be non-bullying issues, *before* initiating the investigation process, and therefore unnecessary to embark on or initiate investigations for in the first place. Nine full school days of lost school counselor support resulted from this half. This is an extreme cost to students in need. The wellness of his students and staff were at stake. He had to do something … radical.

The principal met with his building leadership team and modelled a call to a parent in one of these known non-bullying allegation scenarios. The group had the background to provide contrary evidence to the parent. He spent twenty minutes on the phone with this parent, reviewing the incident, acknowledging a problem existed and explaining how and why this was a matter of conflict that could be resolved through conflict resolution. No formal investigation of bullying was warranted.

Explaining to the parent that this was not a bullying incident, the principal would send an email confirming this, with the understanding that if the incident were to evolve into something more later, the school could and would investigate This left the window open for monitoring and future treatment of issues, accounting for dynamic situations that emerge and removed the necessity to open a formal, drawn out two-week investigation.

A school counselor spent three hours to complete an investigation, between paperwork, student interviews, and documentation.

One phone call took the principal twenty minutes and freed the counselor from hours of paperwork and interviews. He shared a transcript his assistant principals could use to confirm via email to families that they agreed with the determination, and that they could request a follow up, if necessary. A failsafe. A general message stating:

> As per our discussion today regarding an incident you brought to the school's attention, we agree that this is not a bullying incident at this time. Should the circumstances change, you may request a follow up investigation.

His team wondered; *can we do this? Won't we get in trouble? Doesn't this go against district protocol: anytime someone makes a claim, we must investigate*? Administrators are positioned to make leadership decisions. Following a literal path to investigate every allegation is not a leadership decision. It is a bureaucratic one. It is not a radical decision either. Blindly following procedure goes against the grain of true, and courageous leadership. The principal assured his team that the payoff was worth it.

Results

90% of parents contacted with this new approach agreed with the administration's explanation. Taking twenty minutes to show parents the reality of the situation enabled the school to reduce unnecessary battles between warring families, decrease investigations in 9 out of 10 circumstances, and improve school climate. Best of all, students were learning how to manage conflict, rather than handing the problem off to adults. This prevented losing out on a valuable conflict resolution and life-learning experience.

Certainly, true bullying incidents exist, and, when they do, the school must rigorously investigate, and proactively prevent continued or future incidents from resurfacing. In fact, by focusing on legitimate bullying concerns, instead of the unnecessary ones, the school can be more laser-focused, with greater earnestness. The intent of bullying law and school expectations can be realized. School officials can make it count, being authentic and responsive to dealing with substantive school issues.

Was this a risk? Of course, the principal had not consulted his superiors. Yet he knew from experience that this approach would not have been endorsed had he appealed for consideration.

When the Other Shoe Drops…

A year later, the principal received a call from his supervisor. He was asked, "You know that letter you send to parents when they agree it's not a bullying incident?" The principal froze for a moment and then responded cautiously, "yes…?" His superior replied, "Could you send me a copy? I'd like to share it with the other principals, as a model." Waiting for the other shoe to drop, he pulled up the transcript template on his computer, and emailed it instantly.

This simple transcript, and a twenty-minute phone call to many well-intentioned parents who simply need clarification on how an incident with their child had truly transpired, serves as a difference maker in time, school climate and in seeing that radical change can happen from the middle. It can be realized with courage, and the willingness to beg for forgiveness rather than ask for permission.

Summary

Being a radical leader can sound and seem risky. Yet the risk of not taking radical action is far riskier, especially for our most disadvantaged students. Defining Radical Principals: leaders thinking outside the box, being innovative and making change in ways that are courageous, often nudging strategically and boldly beyond the status quo. Being radical is too big a payoff to stay in the status quo. Every child, every underdog must be given opportunity, no exceptions and the Radical Principal must courageously insist on this. This is not easy, but it is simple, if our focus is trained on the right path.

Working around bureaucracy and institutionalized practices that have persisted far beyond their relevance requires strategic approaches and understanding that can allow the Radical Principal to make real change. The hardest challenges are also the most discrete, and the Radical Principal exposes these, before commanding (not demanding) authentic change. We learn about a principal who was challenged by a child regarding the biased language written into his dress code, and how he decided to listen, and make changes to foster a fair, and empowering dress code for all.

A big part of Radical Principals' ability to adapt to change and leverage it for her school's community results from an open mindset, a willingness to step out of our all-knowing mindset and accept that other ideas may, in fact, often come from other people and places. Examples of once-thriving companies who refused to adapt to their circumstances, such as Blackberry, showed why they went from a height of incredible success, free-falling to utter failure. Leaders and their organizations who are open to adaptation avoid this, and students win.

Principals sit in the middle, literally as "middle management," and this can create challenges from both directions in their quest to create radical schools. Sometimes, using their will to take a chance pays off, when they beg for forgiveness, knowing all too well that asking for permission will get them nowhere. Doing so can generate ideas that after already established, superiors must accept as a thriving practice, one that helps all children. Every child, every underdog.

2

How Do I Become Radical?

Personality tests have been popular in schools, in the corporate world, and in therapy professions for decades. People are interested in learning about what their learning styles and preferences are, or to confirm what they believe are their strengths, and areas to work on regarding their self-improvement.

Yet these are not tell-all, conclusive characterizations of an individual, dictating that you must follow the path of a personality profile that has been predestined for you. We are not all fixed in one personality portrait or another. Rather, we lean towards one direction or another, favoring certain qualities, yet also possessing attributes of others. Understanding and recognizing this set of tendencies over end-alls will help school leaders understand what might hold them back from the kind of decision making that distinguishes Radical Principals.

Almost no one is completely extroverted and 100% daring. On the other hand, almost no one is completely introverted, passive and resistant to make radical change. In fact, it is too risky

DOI: 10.4324/9781003275718-2

FIGURE 2.1 Radical Personality Types (Shows That Most Individuals Lean, but Are Still Not All the Way to One Extreme or the Other)

to always be radical, in a literal sense. Likewise, no bold change occurs when individuals are invariably cautious in their decision-making processes (Figure 2.1).

Herein lies the problem with personality assessments and profiles. They are helpful in establishing what our preferences are and yet are prone to being too restrictive when we arrive at preconceived notions about learning preferences. We risk blindly leaning into that tendency. When presented with personality profiles, be conscious of this and assured that this should never inhibit anyone from getting outside of their own limitations.

Additionally, be mindful that radical leadership requires some guiding principles. Being radical does not mean forcing yourself onto the face of an issue or person to make effective change for learners. Extreme measures do not always mean being aggressive. Striking a thoughtful balance to approach decisions is far wiser and more effective. This means being keenly radical in pursuit of effecting true change; maneuvering between taking proactive approaches and engaging in cautious adjustments when each serves the end goal.

Understanding who we are as individuals and as leaders, what limitations and strengths we possess and how to master each of these will help principals be radically competent. Administrators entered educational leadership positions from different doorways. How each arrived is unimportant. What matters is how they manage change, once inside that door. Remaining sheltered in safety on one side, or hazardously in the face of danger on the other does not make us radical. Doing so makes a leader run into destructive obstacles. Job security, or the outcomes of students are put at risk. Then no real radical change can gain momentum.

Approaching values in a calculated way toward radical leadership, it is prudent not to become stagnant in the safer harbor of compliance. Radical Principals have a responsibility to initiate change where institutionalized shelters have stood in the way far too long and must be minimized, replaced, or shifted. Different personality styles are less inclined to be radical in this change process. Varying qualified administrators and educational leaders possess vastly contrasting leadership styles. That is not the issue. Accepting one's limitations as fixed in place is.

While diverse leaders have different styles, they all share a common bond: an aspiration to help children succeed. That is at the core of the value's educational leaders possess. This value alone allows them to speak a common language. Yet some may risk apprehension to reject practices that have shielded more privileged individuals while, at the same time, harboring barriers for opportunity with less privileged students.

It may seem obvious on the surface to reject practices that prevent less advantaged learners from the same opportunities as their peers. We cannot justify submission; we must lead the call to act. Yet the problem is situated in the elusiveness with which inequity can trickle into day-to-day practices and operations. If we do not carefully and actively look consciously and deeply into the unintended biases that persist among many in our school community, even within ourselves, then we will miss a whole world of robust opportunity for children, right underneath our noses, leaving many unfairly behind.

Radical Principals are not necessarily instinctive actors in taking a radical approach to change. The forces that sway a leader to move a school community beyond the norm are often caused by other factors. One strong indicator is with those who may have experienced a tremendous loss or challenge, bringing a realization of values into clear focus and motivating them to act. This may be likened to an awakening, a deeper meaning, even a calling.

Educational leaders tend to be quite disciplined, intelligent, successful, and … safe. Many of them know what works and are inclined to stick with more conservative methods. Although what works affords opportunities for some, safe processes do not work for many children. They are most often the students in greatest need of leaders who engage in the kind of radical decision-making provided in this guide.

When an educator thinks and acts outside the norm, they can see with a clearer vision, the need to push against convention. Yet what can be costly is that others, those in positions of authority and influence may likely view the Radical Principal's actions as noncompliance. Innovative ways of remastering social structures within schools foster opportunities for all and change a culture for the better, for everyone. Everyone wins. Yet, all of this comes at a risk.

Bold educators may not make it far enough along in the recruitment process to become educational leaders, administrators, and, ultimately, Radical Principals. Even if they pursue these avenues, they are often redirected or denied opportunities to grow because they do not fit a mold of leadership envisioned by those deciding who fits. They are often viewed as rebels who do not follow district protocols and guidelines.

Therefore, many, if not most who make it to school leadership-level positions are those who have adapted with a methodology of compliance. They crossed their T's and dotted their I's. When they were asked to read the code of conduct to the class as a reminder of what good behavior was, they did, rather than asking why we do this. They nodded with vigorous affirmation when their superior inquired, how did the kids respond? *Do you think we got our point across?* Yes, they got the message!

Compliance does not foster creativity, nor does it enhance ingenuity. Conformity comes at a cost for those who lose as a consequence, students and particularly those most in need of radical ingenuity. This is because teaching children through actions and modeling can and should empower them to see and understand in ways that are far more persuasive than lecturing to them and reading the code of conduct.

If many administrators made it as far as they did by staying within their lane, how then could we possibly expect them to consider acting with radical decisiveness? How do we get them to contemplate making big changes, shifting processes to address student circumstances, especially when they must also navigate frequent bureaucratic obstacles? Acknowledging the ever-present inequities that exist, administrators must aspire to see beyond the horizon, in a balance of progressive, calculated, and visionary ways.

This text proposes that for both lifelong rule followers and those rebellious enough who made it past the checkpoints, they can be focused on creativity by adopting various strategies, to enable all Radical Principals to engineer important change in their schools. This happens through incremental and strategic steps that have long term, compounding long-lasting effects that shift toward opportunities for all within the school community.

A Caution

This is not to say that Radical Principals or other educators should categorically refuse legal, or district-mandated, procedures and guidelines. Rather, they should question the status quo, especially if the current state of affairs appears to be harming children, and of greater consequence, if those who suffer are already at a disadvantage. Like the principal who wondered about a dated dress code after one student challenged him, implementing a measured and adaptable approach is what creates the change necessary for all to benefit.

Understanding that this is of far greater consequence than one may fully realize, radical leaders can begin to think deeply about the purpose of longstanding roles and expectations. Why are they in place? Who do they serve? How can I be a part of the change that serves as a catalyst to resolve long standing barriers, once and for all?

Being Radical Is Messy, and That's a Good Thing

It has been established that many educators are rule followers, who tend to stay out of troubled waters, and are those who remain comfortably within a safe zone. Yet stepping outside of protective shelters can produce incredible results and change for a school community that frees them from the bonds that limit the potential for remarkable success, for all. This is messy for educators. They are asked to organize thoughtful lesson plans, strategize curriculum, arrange schedules and events, run class changes, and manage lunch supervision. Doesn't this seem to go against the grain of the systematic rule and order in schools as institutions?

Taking risks can feel chaotic for those expected to lead a safe and orderly school environment. Organizing patterns of rules and guidelines seems sensible enough. The educator who creates the best syllabus may likely be the same professional who struggles with being messy.

Indeed, the very strengths that so many teachers are recruited for and survive with long term are the ones that do not get them to push for innovation. They are too risky; reckless. Yet, if educators can shift some of their understanding toward being more open and innovative to new opportunities, they will experience less dismay from inhibiting their mental energy (Soto, 2018) and drive toward a perspective that reinforces the kinds of transformation that propel schools toward radical change.

Let's look at being messy from another perspective. Consider messiness as a form of controlled chaos. This is familiar to those learning a new skill. Educators are well positioned as experts in their subject area. They spend years cultivating their craft. This is pragmatic when mastering an area of content in enabling teachers to provide instruction for students to learn from a strong foundation. After all, to know the content assures far fewer errors in instruction. Yet consider why a Beginner's Mindset can serve everyone, and especially, the experts.

Beginner's Mindset was part of an earlier topic and is worth exploring in further detail related to teacher styles and their impact on learners. The concept of a Beginner's Mindset is a conscious willingness toward openness, enthusiasm, and of eliminating assumptions when learning a skill. This is perhaps especially important as a mindset when engaging in advanced study or understanding.

A Beginner's Mindset offers the willingness to absorb new or differing (even conflicting) information, acting like a sponge, soaking in all the information, just as a beginner's mind might naturally do. Remember the excitement of children exploring and learning when considering this approach. A sense of unabated discovery stimulates excitement and enthusiasm for the learner.

There is remarkable advantage to approaching experiences as a neophyte, even if you already know, or think you know a great deal about a subject. It makes a person more inclined to experiment, to question the current situation, to explore options that would have otherwise been eliminated due to knowing one way just good enough. This has the potential to open windows into ideas and solutions that present new and ground-breaking paths toward a solution.

A helpful way to persuade experienced educators about implementing an open mindset is to remind them that learners are constantly experiencing a beginner's mindset. Indeed, they benefit their students greatly (and themselves) by modeling their willingness toward an open learning model. Possibilities are nearly endless with a beginner's mind, yet they become limited to a very small fraction of prospects when we view ourselves as all-knowing, experienced, seasoned, and not needing to add to or adapt to our repertoire.

Viewing oneself as an "expert" substantially disrupts the likelihood of radical ideology, of willing examination to new and even speculative discoveries and approaches. This reduces the possibility of educational enlightenment educators may expose students to. Choosing flexibility enables individuals to have a willingness to concede to alternatives that present new methods, creative ideas, and, yes, messy opportunities. This can feel unsettling for educators accustomed to the comfort of their existing knowledge, a familiarity that has stuck with them for a considerable length of time, and likely worked well enough.

Additional techniques for persuading experts to explore their own willingness to be messy, to be open to a Beginner's Mindset are examined. This is especially true with those who are longstanding educators in their content area, or capacity. There are resources that speak greatly to a Beginner's Mindset, and to the value of this approach for learners, professionals, and individuals at any stage of their lives. Ironically, these become more significant with greater influence, and Radical Principals have the potential to seize on this.

Somewhat surprisingly, there is very little guidance on this subject for educators. Yet consider that educators may offer the best resource for radical change in education, and for influencing the exploration of the youth that they teach. Indeed, teaching about the value of a beginners' mindset further encourages openness toward creativity and the expansion of ideas that can truly shift schools away from stagnantly institutionalized practices.

One way is to share about well-known individuals who have experienced incredible success. Consider those who are most triumphant in their area of expertise. Perhaps they have shattered record after record, or simply far exceeded expectations held by others. These individuals often exhibit a humble disposition about their undeniable success. They speak more of what they must work on to improve their craft, and how their surroundings afforded them success in their remarkable achievement, rather than on their own merits. They are not *done learning*.

Illustrating these examples from the greats, in athletics, in corporate contexts and in education are concrete reference points for educators to recognize in thinking about an open mindset among the great success stories. Talk to Teacher of the Year recipients and you will hear little about how or why they are so great. Instead, you will hear how much they must improve, and how they credit much of their success to other people and factors:

> This award really belongs to the 1500 + students I have served in public education, to my husband for being an ear and soundboard for me within the ins and outs of each day of each academic year, and the teachers around me that help build a community that is focused on continuously improving our standards, our strategies, and our practices…
>
> (Hampton, 2021)

> This award is not about the recognition of an individual, it is the recognition of a community. Each of us, administrators, family members, parents, staff and teachers make up that community. The whole is far greater than any one part.
>
> (Schwerdt, n.d.)

As you can see from these testimonies from highly successful, accomplished teachers, a recognition of lifelong learning, about how others played a more pivotal role and an acknowledgement that they have so much more to aspire to is highlighted. They cite how much they must learn and gain (Wessling, 2014), acknowledging that their success was more a credit to their acceptance of best practices like a Beginner's Mindset (flexible), rather than to some innate (fixed) talent. There are two important points of emphasis about teaching with a Beginner's Mindset:

1. Great teachers maintain a Beginner's Mindset because they see through the noise and chaos of systems and directly into the heart of what truly matters.

2. You can only become great when you do not see yourself as great, because if you let go of that beginner's mindset, that propels a relentless pursuit toward growth and possibility, you are letting go of what keeps you aspiring. You are giving up on the very tool that propels you to move toward supporting student success without this mindset.

This mark of modesty about one's success, an approach of unassuming acknowledgement toward openness for new ideas, is a pillar in the foundation for radical change in school leadership. It can materialize from any corner of the school. The Radical Principal is prepared to remain adaptable, to practice the Beginner's Mindset, to encourage and model radical ideas from her faculty. This kind of willingness opens the door for true and pivotal change, the sort that invigorates a school community to pursue even more. It allows them to explore in ways that energizes and innovates for all. That is progress, that is radical, and that's when kids win.

Summary

Everyone has traits that lean toward one style or another, but no one is all one trait or another, and every leader can become more resilient in their ability to adapt their traits to become more radical. Understanding who leaders are, and how their strengths and limitations position them, helps develop this resilience. This understanding and willingness allows educational leaders to avoid extreme, career ending risk and not sit in neutral, resisting the call for change to help children.

Being conscious of our limitations, and embracing our strengths allows radical leaders to discard, shift, or minimize those practices that have somehow sustained beyond the point of absurd, that harm children, especially those most in need of radical change. Regardless of personality type, all school leaders must have as their core principle to help children in need, and that becomes more urgent for disadvantaged children. Radical leaders carefully and actively look consciously and deeply into the unintended biases that persist among many in our school community, and then act as agents of change to cleverly shift these institutionalized practices.

Compliance does not foster creativity, nor ingenuity, and that comes at a cost for those who lose as a result, students and particularly those most in need. Many leaders gain their position by following the rules and that means they can be less inclined to be radical. Being aware helps, and then understanding the maneuvering techniques that work, sometimes proactively, sometimes along the sidelines is what works for radical school leaders.

Being radical is messy, and that is a good thing. Radical Principals must be prepared for the controlled chaos that is inevitable when we act as agents of unconventional change. Strategies and approaches are presented. Viewing oneself as an "expert" drastically reduces the likelihood of radical ideology, of open examination to new and even speculative discoveries and approaches to consider. The most successful in any incredible journey often possess a humbling, quieting influence. They speak more of what they must work on to improve, and credit others in achieving remarkable success. They are not done learning.

The Radical Principal is prepared to remain open, to practice the beginner's mindset, to encourage and model radical ideas from others, in ways that opens the door for true change.

3

Radical Timing and Stacking

The next two chapters focus on the quantitative and qualitative factors that enable school leaders to be radical by optimizing time (quantitative) and efficiency (qualitative). While these are connected in the leader's overall pursuit to achieve radical change in school communities, they are worthy of separate but equal examination.

One of the most overlooked aspects of generating opportunities to gain an advantage is the element of timing. Understanding the power of *when* to implement an idea can be as or more significant then why, or how. Being able to leverage the underlying patterns of timing to expand on a goal or accomplish something reaps disproportionately high dividends, presenting extraordinary windows of opportunity.

These windows open and shut in a revolving manner, allowing a chance to get through one if the timing is right. They are also rarely shut or open permanently. Allowing these windows to close in the wrong moments or to evade our recognition to

DOI: 10.4324/9781003275718-3

embrace them can generate adverse conditions that reduce or eliminate the possibility for radical change to happen.

Timing can be impactful; in the shorter phases we seek to achieve a goal, in accomplishing something substantial, within incremental minutes and moments. Longer-term phases of timing, such as slower, gradual shifts can be far more sustaining than the adverse conditions that rushed, premature decisions result in. Ideas become better rooted with the proper investment in value for time. Individuals within an organization are often not ready for a rapid shift. Allowing change to move through more strategically, in the right context has massive benefits.

Consider the challenge faced by leaders in attempting to engage in radical change. Bridges (2022) explains how the transition of organizations is connected to change, and when and why they succeed, or fail. He refers to change as not being the cause of challenge to overcome. Rather, it is the transition, or nexus between what once was, the comfort and knowledge of familiar practices or systems, and the unknown that is yet to come. That space between the familiar and unfamiliar is what is so unsettling, so daunting for persons within the organization to make the leap toward. Recognizing this and exploring ways to bridge the gap are how the most effective, radical leaders enact important and positive changes.

Dan Pink (2019) dedicated a whole text to timing elements and weaved scientific concepts together with anecdotal evidence to illustrate everything from the energy cycles of the day to the longer time periods in a person's life. He condensed these into the fundamentals of timing. For the purpose of enacting radical change it is these moments, both short and long term, that are often overlooked and underestimated. When they can be recognized and harnessed, incredible outcomes have the potential to take root.

Radical accomplishments do not take place with one grandiose idea. In the right moments, Radical Principals are wise to engage in multiple maneuvers across different directions. Knowing *when* to apply the right technique is as impactful as knowing how or why. The impact of timing for strategy implementation can come as a surprise to even the most practiced school leader. The significance has enormous implications. Understanding this is a step toward achieving more massive, radical gains.

Consider an instance of timing and decision-making: a principal who was engaged in an intense planning meeting while being alerted that a child was in the hallway, on the floor, violently shaking from the effects of a seizure. There are moments in which radical leaders must step in, act, enlist support staff. and help a child. Immediately, no matter what the circumstance.

There are no exceptions to this scenario. While a disruption to an important planning meeting is inconvenient and can interrupt the flow educational leaders aspire to, this is one of those exceptions. It is imperative to urgently respond to help a child who is in danger. This is nonnegotiable in our protection and care of all children.

On the other hand, there are moments during a school day that should never take a principal away from his broader focus and flow. Being mindful of and understanding such energy-draining and costly circumstances carry far greater weight for the administrator than she may realize in the immediate. Additionally, as significant, is how to manage these nuanced circumstances. What separates a truly radical school leader from ordinary ones is the ability to differentiate these and to insist that they be managed based on true necessity (there are few such principals) and non-immediate follow-up (the majority of school leaders).

Consider one scenario that helps to illustrate this point. In this instance, teachers are upset with their supervisor, because they normally have a week longer to input data required for monitoring their students' progress. The supervisor has insisted that teachers meet her unexpectedly accelerated timeline. What do they do? Come to the principal.

This is not a decision that needs to be rushed, nor answered quickly, as the teachers request with a perceived urgency. There is, in fact, another two weeks before this decision must be acted on. Gather information, find out why. Perhaps there was a change in broader deadlines. Possibly there is a misunderstanding. The principal should almost never let this kind of issue overtake his focus or disrupt his agenda. In the right time and place, information can be gathered, and a response can be made with an informed, measured approach.

Orchestrating radical timing must be a clever and courageous dance; combined with proper packaging and delivery of the idea. Taken together, a series of well-timed yet boldly applied programs and processes allow the Radical Principal to shift momentum in the right direction. This thrusts everyone in the school community forward, toward more effective, pragmatic, and positive change.

Personalizing Radical Timing

Successful leaders are not simply carved out of one make and model, and there is no one cookie cutter for success. We must be prepared to recognize our personalized timing elements, and how they work. These differ based on the individual. We should be highly reflective on what timing elements work best and how and when bad timing affects our work progress. It is then that we can shape our work around goals, forging the elements of timing across best practices.

Consider three lessons about timing that aid leadership self-awareness. These enable the Radical Principal to structure professional (and personal) life in far more efficient, and productive ways. Following are the ways that differentiate how:

1. A person's emotions run through cyclical patterns that are surprisingly predictable, each day.

2. Knowing the way you function will help you do your best work.
3. Taking a break and delaying further work is not inefficient. In fact, preserving time for restoration helps you save time.

Emotional Patterns

A study by Cornell University analyzed hundreds of millions of tweets. The results revealed several common cyclical patterns for most individuals that are worth demonstrating why it is so instrumental to calibrate for radical timing:

1. *Morning peak*. Most people feel pretty good early in the day, regardless of how slow or fast of a start they start with. This is the time of day when (where possible) it is best to invest in creative, high-level cognitive thought processes. Your brain is well rested, and at a high functional peak of efficiency. You may find using this time for important visionary meetings, and planning discussions ideal to align your schedule to.
2. *Afternoon low*. You know how difficult it is to stay awake after lunch? That low point in the day is not just in your head. There is a physiological response that impacts how you react. Understanding this allows school leaders to minimize (where possible) those moments when they engage in high level discussion and thought.

   Instead, use this time to address more nominal, mundane tasks. You may find using this time to check email, follow up on procedural chores such as orders, signing off on items, and visiting the hallways and classrooms to be a few of the less cognitively demanding ways you can engage in at a lower, less cognitively demanding gear.

3. *Evening rebound*. Once you finish your workday, even the most grueling day will take a turn. As the day winds down, seize the moments that enable you to diagnose and correct problems. Being aware of this and knowing your time will come serves as an opportunity to clean up some tasks that got you pulled away when you depart that morning peak, distracted by the afternoon blues.

Kahneman (2012) reinforces this rationale for patterns of timing. If we know that for most of us, this kind of sequence in our day endures, we should establish a framework that is organized to suit our efficiency modes throughout the day. By becoming highly self-regulatory, we are maximizing our ability to exert the best energy in the most impactful way, and at the most congruent times.

Understanding and structuring these timing intervals where possible frees individuals from the struggle of performing tasks at less efficient times and allows them to optimize time and energy at the most advantageous production peaks possible. Additionally, we can bring ourselves back to more effective states, if we understand the self-regulatory mechanisms that allow us to train our focus. More follows about how to manage low points and to induce high points on command in the upcoming chapter on radical communication.

Stacking and Timing

The alignment of timing is a factor that is even more significant when the strategy of stacking is adopted. Stacking involves incorporating multiple ideas, strategies, and techniques, running across each other in ways that offer a menu of options for educators to draw on as access points to create multiple possibilities. Stacking creates an additive effect that, over time, results in an exponentially magnifying set of beneficial results. Idea stacking forges an interaction that amplifies and compounds the benefits of focus and flow.

Radical Principals can leverage their understanding through stacking to expand the results of success in a trajectory that produces a disproportionately larger payoff than what was invested. Piling strategies on top of each other expands and hastens the response time for many students in need. Creating this interaction takes the various techniques, coordinated together, and fosters a compound effect (Gaskell, 2021).

Stacking techniques substantially increases the likelihood that helping many students, more often will perpetuate their success. This enhances how often learners will improve and thrive. Acknowledge that while not all students gain from an additive effect, offering this in a consolidated format helps far more students, intensifying the effect, and netting a value that cannot be reproduced when offering solutions in silos. The more integrated, the greater the composite effect from combining methods together. While standalone ideas may work, they will remain far more limited in scope.

Short-term impact can validate this effect with impressive and significantly noticeable results. Another factor in stacking is the longer-term, synergistic set of outcomes. Consider scientific evidence that *space is curved*. There are no such things as straight lines—everything, including one's own life trajectory, is curved.

A person's daily choices determine which curve they are situated on. If they are making the right choices most days and moments, their life curve is on an upper trend. If, on the other hand, they are making simple errors in judgment more frequently than the right choices, they are on a downward curve. These curves accelerate with momentum and time.

Since life is curved, and so are the implications of our decisions, there is no standing still. A person is either moving forward, or moving backward; up or down. Radical timing offsets the imbalance of those occasions where, by human nature, we all take a step in reverse. Creating more moments in an upward curve generates a steady, if not choppy upward path. This becomes exponentially greater over time, and starts to unleash remarkable results if consistently, not perfectly moving in that upward and curved direction.

Consider this from another perspective: a 1% improvement every day (1% + 1% + 1%…) for a year leads to a 365% improvement. This simple mathematical calculation allows us to compute and recognize the likelihood of direction we take. Applying the concept of radical timing, we can harness momentum to gain more consolidated progressions of success that accumulate over time, in disproportionately higher milestones. The same is true with regression. Being cognizant of this equips the radical leader with the knowledge to enable them to benefit from directional timing.

Replication can certainly be practiced when stacking techniques together, with the knowledge that adaptations are not only an option for your school context; they should be expected in the process of radical progress. Educators are wise to borrow ideas that seem to be working quite well in other communities, schools, classrooms, and organizations. Being prepared to adopt the parts that fit their school context is as important as remaining flexible enough to adjust to unique circumstances.

Adaptation and flexibility play an important role in acting as a radical leader. It calls for the ability to maneuver in ways that allow for a focused, yet flexible approach. Successful leaders engage in this important trait of adaptability. Yet, like many of the practices presented on leadership success, very little originates from the educational realm or prominently exists there. Instead, it is borrowed from business and corporate contexts. It is for this reason that references presented here are synthesized from evidenced practices beyond schools, balanced with anecdotal evidence to serve the environments of educational institutions.

One example is the *versatility* to frame the flexible and adaptable leadership and thinking approach (Kaiser, 2020). Versatility reinforces the need to remain visionary in leadership exploration and curiosity, keeping the same open mind previously mentioned, and in maintaining a willingness to bend and adapt.

Understanding this is often what distinguishes the radical leader from the "just-good-enough" manager.

Radical timing also involves how and when leaders engage their minds. In a constantly "on" world, one educational leader vividly recalls the first time he went radio silent, because of the profound impact it had on his mindset when he returned from the quiet solitude of structured focus to his busy daily world.

He was scheduled to go on a cruise over the summer, prior to a seasonal school opening and discovered soon after getting on board that he would not have access to cellular data. Worried at first that he might miss something important, after a day cruising, he realized how incredibly liberating being offline, and radio silent was. At peace and separated from the negative news cycles and cynicism of the outside world, he could quiet his mind, and recalibrate.

Arriving back in port days later, he resumed having data access, amid an influx of emails and messages pinging and updating his phone. He addressed these one by one; learning that many were questions and problems that had already been resolved or issued that had subsided. He also realized if someone truly needed him, they could have reached him in an emergency. Even on a cruise, he still had that very basic accessibility.

This "offline" lesson was invaluable as a learning experience for this educational leader: to re-energize by going off-grid. Since then, he has traveled to Europe, and stateside. With phone in hand, he now takes manual steps, by removing professional email accounts from his device while away, and applying the Do Not Disturb feature. In fact, this kept him from replying reflexively to offensive, challenging or combative messages. He returned primed to respond more effectively for a better outcome for a child; reminded that in the end, that was all that mattered in radical schools.

Using this strategy, the school leader is able to be recharged and ready to go when back to the grindstone. There is a misnomer in leadership, within the United States especially, that we must always be "on". In other Western nations, such as Europe, it is common to remain away, off, and offline for weeks at a time for this important reason. Recovery is as critical as work time, and radical timing is optimized when we restore and rest.

A few practical tips: Always set an away message first, and then slow down to the reality and tranquility around that helps prime the mind. Use the Do Not Disturb feature. These make for more constructive time with family and friends, as leaders discover how to value being more in tune with what's going on around them instead of being distracted by ongoing digital disruptions. Educators can reverse the symptoms of the hyperactive mind. This taxes primary instincts and energy resources, rather than helping to restore and rest to regain needed energy and focus.

When you do something that feels important now but discover later that it almost never is, this becomes a much more hazardous form of distraction because you have permitted distraction to deceive you into prioritizing the urgent at the cost of the essential. Remember that phrase, *the urgent at the cost of the essential*. Allowing these distractions inhibits the leader's capacity to elevate into visionary, long term, and productive achievement capacities, tied to energy cycles. When you stay always-on even as you do not truly need to, you evade the opportunities born of solitude that allow for achievement at higher levels.

Remember the winners: Children. Radio silence reaps benefits for those most in need of the school leaders' time and focus. Energy cycles are optimized when adjusting to this restorative approach. These breaks are what will help school leaders achieve for children at their best, and they deserve, in fact, demand your time, focus and energy.

Summary

To act radically, a school leader should be keenly aware of the element of timing. Often in our busy day-to-day functions, this is overlooked and while there is cause, we should take care to address the qualitative and quantitative aspects of timing to enlist more significant ways to accomplish radically. The uncomfortable space between what was and what can be is the area most challenging to push radical change through.

In the right moments, Radical Principals are wise to wage multiple maneuvers at the same time. This causes the compounding benefit of stacking. Priority infrequently trumps timing, but when it does, it is always about the welfare of children. What separates a truly radical school leader from every other is the ability to differentiate these and to insist that they be managed based on true urgency (these are few) or follow-up (these are most).

Well-timed, yet boldly applied programs and processes allow the Radical Principal to shift momentum in the right direction, where true change happens. Timing is also a personalized ideology that should be understood and then mastered for individually maximized achievement. A tremendous amount of consistency exists regarding timing, as confirmed in a global study, so this should serve as a guide.

Radical leaders should establish a framework that is organized to suit our efficiency modes throughout the day. By becoming highly self-regulatory, we maximize our energy use. Stacking allows multiple strategies, and techniques, running across each other to offer options that enable educators to draw on those multiple possibilities. Stacking techniques substantially increase the likelihood that helping many students, more often will increase who succeeds, and how often. Stacking in an upward curve generates a larger output over time, for student success.

Radical school leaders must be adaptable, maneuvering to continue enhancing benefits for their school. Finding ways to be offline can be regenerative when breaks allow for this. We should proactively take advantage of these opportunities. Don't allow distraction to deceive you into prioritizing the urgent at the cost of the essential. Protect your creative moments, through planned moments of radio silence and students will be the real victors.

4

Radical Efficiency

Get Everything You Can Out of All You've Got

Radical efficiency involves the management of ideas, and challenges in ways that turn Radical Principals toward qualitative productivity. This efficiency preserves the leader's ability to harness practices that work remarkably well, versus the humdrum of frustrating experiences that when implemented, provoke resistance and exasperation. That's neither qualitative nor efficient. Consider the kind of interference that prevents us from managing with this manner of radical efficiency, which are then followed by methods to counter fruitless obstacles.

Sourcing Work Out to Increase Productivity

The school leader's efficiency can be too significantly impaired due to expectations that attention calls for in an overcrowded set of demands. Therefore, leaders should protect opportunities at all costs. Circumstances determine how they forgo their efficiency, when it is warranted and ethically demanded for. For instance,

DOI: 10.4324/9781003275718-4

upon discovering that a student had been molested by a step-parent, one principal knew that offering his time, energy and empathy to the biological parent was not only important but was also his ethical and moral obligation. This was one of those radical leadership moments that are prioritized above all.

The administrator spent an hour with this parent, consoling, counseling and assuring her. He vividly recalls a few days later when the affected student stopped by his office to say she wanted to thank him for being so nice to her mom. After all this child had been through, she thought it important to reach out to the principal for consoling her parent. Moments like these are both chilling and tear jerking, and they occur randomly. They are the occasions radical leaders give top priority and attention to, and at all costs.

At other times, there are mundane tasks to be fulfilled by the principal, and most of these should be sourced to other, reliably competent individuals. Principals need their attention and attention aimed at radical improvement, not the tedium of distraction. Their school community cannot afford to lay waste to this, but too often, many often do. When confronting this, delegate as much and as responsibly as possible.

One example occurred in a school community where security was known to be a priority. While that was a wonderful comfort to the principal, there was one item that should not have been an unnecessary and time-consuming burden to her. Central office administrators had assigned her to meticulously inventory the walkie talkie allotment at her school, and document this tracking on hard copy files, each and every school week. In a small school, with a few office-only walkie talkies, this may not have been much of a time commitment. However, in a large school such as this one, there were dozens of radios, housed in numerous departments and wings, throughout her large secondary school campus.

Fully inventorying these took over an hour weekly. That kind of process is an unacceptable use of a school leader's time, which would be better allocated to acting as a radical leader. What did she do? The principal assigned this task to a trustworthy clerical staff member and instructed her how to properly inventory the radios. All that had to be done was to sign the hard copy sheets weekly, which took a few brief moments. This meant that her school community was given back 36 hours of radical leadership productivity over a school year. That kind of time and service dedication should always remain preserved and nonnegotiable.

This principal attempted to highlight the loss in valued visionary time to her superiors and was met with dismissive disregard. Do it (!) was the refrain. This response is all too common, but the answer by our principal was a clever way to re-establish an efficiency and focus that her school community and disadvantaged children call for. When you are drowning in bureaucracy, be inventive. It is always better to beg for forgiveness, than to ask for permission for time better spent supporting children in need over attending to low level menial tasks.

Connecting Non-Teaching Staff to Kids

One of the most significant changes in recent history has been the addition and expansion of security in schools. They are fortified in ways that make them look and feel very different than just a quarter-century ago. This is certainly important as school communities need to carry on with important business without fear of danger to student and faculty safety.

For schools to genuinely flourish, they must first be havens where children can effectively escape the ravages of the outside world, especially if their world has placed them at peril. Entering schools that set this tone enables the children to have the benefit of gearing their mind and body toward higher-order thinking and learning, just as Radical Principals strive to model for them. Primal defenses can be shed, and tangible developmental opportunities become prospects to engage in thriving learning experiences.

As the presence of security has increased, the role of staff members assigned to secure schools has become intertwined within the campus. Some have integrated remarkably well and worked to diminish the biases influencing generations of families that may unfortunately prevail between law enforcement and less privileged families. Right or wrong, this is a reality that must be confronted and doing so effectively has undeniable advantages for the entire school community.

One school achieved this by crafting a program which allowed students to engage in behavioral learning opportunities with retired police officers. It served as a platform to frame relationships as mentor–mentee. This altered the perception of many who may have held biased perceptions, and positive outcomes became too significant to assume they were coincidental. It is well worth sharing here because it was such an invaluable lesson and easily replicable.

Consider the power this offers learners who fear those representing law enforcement as a chance to adjust their view, and for adult mentors to do the same. This has extraordinary implications beyond the school community, and among young learners. When a child returns home and shares their experience with family, a security officer advocated for them in a positive and caring way, mindsets begin to shift. This initiates the cycle of reversing perceptions through simplistic and recurring communication patterns that flow in both directions.

School security, often retired law enforcement officers, are given the chance to support a child, to be a model for a young life, and to see them through a different lens as someone they are invested in, as a mentee. Like teachers, almost every police officer who retires and returns to work in schools has chosen to do so because they are committed to helping children. In this context, we can truly seize on fruitful and vibrant relationship opportunities between students, staff, and families.

The school is able to provide structural conditions to enable this, and the results are extremely rewarding for all. Having security officers serve in this supportive way, the school effectively and efficiently reduces discipline, as suspension rates fall fast, and a school climate warms, offering a welcoming learning environment for all.

Security officers build relationships, instead of walls when mentoring children. While a security officer's first duty is to ensure the safety and security of all within the school building, they make monumental advances in doing so by establishing relationships with children who face disadvantages. Instituting this may sound radical. It most certainly is. By now, you may guess that that is the idea.

This sets the tone with safer, more pleasant schools for all. Mentoring programs disrupt stubbornly gridlocked communication gaps between law enforcement and the less privileged. This interrupts cycles of blame and finger pointing and replaces it with a caring, supportive, and trusting relationship that permeates the entire school.

How to Bring This to Your School

Non-punitive alternatives to suspension, like one middle school that conceptualized this idea, are referred to as the *schoolhouse adjustment* (eSchool Media Contributors, 2018). With this program, students are offered an alternative to discipline. Making this voluntary provides the incentive of choice and with choice is power. Being able to decide on their own is an important part of getting students and their families on board.

The program is a terrific sales pitch for parents of children who are often eager to try anything other than the same old punishment that has not worked for their child and, right or wrong, may be perceived as unjust. The security officer meets with the student, discusses alternative choices to their behavior and, as importantly, takes time to build relationships with the child, focusing on the future, not the past.

Interventions are documented and data on students receiving the intervention are tracked, representing significant reductions in both suspension and repeat disciplinary infractions. Follow-up conferences help advance the relationship into an ongoing and rewarding mentoring relationship.

Like any successful program, the schoolhouse adjustment does not work for every child, all the time. Instead, patterns of steady progress emerge, and these stand out as models for a broader level of achievement. This program clearly makes a difference. How was a once-improbable bond between school security and disadvantaged children shaped? One student and intervention at a time. It is a worthy alternative to ineffective disciplinary consequences.

The communication link established between security and students sustains throughout and schools are better places due to the long-term effects of a bond shaped by replacing punishment with support and consequence with intervention, resulting in noticeable schoolwide changes that forges a safer, warmer climate for all. This is especially true for disadvantaged children, and adults whose biases are further diminished. Security views children they work with in a mentoring capacity in a different light rather than in a punitive role, resulting in a win-win circumstance.

Quieting the Hyperactive Hive Mind

A principal was driving to school one quiet morning, in mid-December when the darkness persisted past 7:00 a.m. adding to the solitude of a late predawn winter morning. That is, until he received a text message that would alter the trajectory of his whole day, and week ahead.

The message had made its way to his phone, migrating through a series of messaging exchanges. It contained a threat to "shoot up the school," and specified a date, which was listed as the previous day. Although dated, safety protocols were promptly implemented, as the school leader consulted his security team and local law enforcement. Meanwhile before he could sit down at his desk to inform the school community about the investigation, he and his school became inundated by misinformation bombarding the social media landscape.

In under an hour, it was confirmed that no credible threat existed, and that this post had originated from an unrelated town and school community. "This was not our school's story,' he outlined quite plainly in a communication with his school, detailing the facts. Assuming that should have been the end of it would have been a mistake. Rumors spread quickly, despite the clear factual message discrediting any present danger. Parents were racing to the school, urgently picking up their children, and faculty were unsettled with how to respond to the confusion.

The principal sent an additional message to his faculty, asking them to reinforce the facts, again reiterating that this was not their story, that it belonged to another town, school, and day, and that it was time to move on. He was accustomed to being trusted by his school community and the persistence of rumors regardless of his repeated assurances clarifying the reality concerned him. What went wrong? What was going on?

Later in the week, a similar, even more ambiguous threat permeated the social media stratosphere, and the school was again barraged with disruptive, escalating interruptions and confusion. It felt like the bad plot of a horror movie, where you can't kill off the crazy ax murderer, no matter how many times you try. These inaccurate and dangerous rumors persisted beyond reason. It ultimately resulted in a paralysis of logical thought and focus across the school community.

Leaders who strive to engage in radical efficiency take on the enemy of efficiency, which is often the irrational reactions of others or of other circumstances, driven by fear and emotion. They strike a balance between empathy for the concern and, simultaneously, radiate the confidence people need to feel assured that all will be well.

School leaders must apply tactics that uncover the truth, and help people regain an authentic and sensible perspective. Misinformation is the dangerous product of an online feedback loop. Rantings of conspiracy theorists sharing amateur analysis in their social media echo chambers are the result of viral social media misinformation.

Algorithms within social media platforms are designed to drive more of the same news to people, fueling their increased link to an information source, no matter how off-base it is. This is accomplished by mirroring our expectations. It embodies a deceiving confirmation bias that perpetually reinforces assumptions by the consumer.

Misinformation must be confronted across multiple fronts. This is not to minimize tragedy that has increased understandable alarm in schools. Any one potential or actual tragedy is too many. Real disasters are not social media misinformation, and this problem must be acknowledged. However, there is often a disproportionate response to the reality of a situation. For instance, heightening security is a typical response that is not the proactive, nor long-term solution. Proactively addressing school climate is.

Any tragedy is horrific but they are also factually farther and fewer in frequency than our perceptions trick us into believing. Providing a steady stream of truth for teachers, students and families allows for more ways to shift groupthink to the positive, and to reduce the chaos and confusion of social media misinformation into more objective lenses of reality.

The issue of misinformation is nothing new. Propaganda had been a threat long before the challenges of social media. Digital access further amplifies voices to reach farther and speak louder into a digital megaphone. This greater reach causes the misinformation to spread faster than leaders and fact-based agents have been able to respond to.

Teaching our students, families, and faculty ways to fight social media misinformation is a big part of the answer, because it is a preemptive strike that enables them to be better prepared to manage misinformation when it inundates them. How do we redirect our school communities toward a more focused, productive mindset that effectively evades the constant bombardment and disruptions of social media misinformation? How do we alter the path to become radical school communities that foster more enhanced learning and growth opportunities for students?

Calming the Hyperactive Hive Mind in Schools

The increased attention on school violence is understandably unnerving. This has generated a disproportionate and compounded response when potential threats are reported. Radical leaders must actively project perspective to adjust the hyperactive hive mind and offset the power of misinformation. Take the time to recalibrate a community's mindset, flipping it instead, toward a group state of flow.

Dispel Illusions by Pointing to the Proof

Tell the truth: Facts visibly show that students have a far lower risk of harm in their school by a weapon, than almost any other mortality risk they face, including *traveling to and from school*, catching a *potentially deadly* disease in school and suffering a life-threatening injury playing interscholastic sports (Ropeik, 2018). This is reality, even as recent events might cause us to assume otherwise and blaring this reality loudly to offset fictional narratives helps.

Parents are strongly linked to their children, biasing their logic in ways that cause an emotional and illogical reaction, one that overrides sense and sensibility. We assess the damage resulting from something as attention-grabbing as a school shooting less on the probability of the consequence and more on the nature of the experience involved that results in its tragic outcome.

To put it another way, the odds of students being victimized by school violence are almost zero, even as issues have appeared to accelerate. The true number can be characterized as falling into the extremely rare category. There is no disputing this data and broadcasting these facts to replace misinformation can offset an exaggerated assumption of fear.

Understanding the strong emotional bond parents have for their children, and the extreme exaggerations about school violence disproportionately (and inaccurately) make the risk feel far greater than it actually is. We act, compelled by our feelings, to protect children. Not seeing reality because of this overpowering emotion is a powerful contradiction, something referred to as the *awareness heuristic*.

The awareness heuristic helps us understand why a disproportionate discrepancy in logic drives fear, whether it is perceived harm to a school community, or the near-zero chance of a plane crash. This means we generate a mental shortcut to rapidly measure the expected rate of things too big for us to truly understand. This produces a highly inaccurate and often overstated narrative in our head.

The more readily an incident is drawn into our frame of mind from recall, the more persistently something becomes newsworthy, the more emotionally prevailing and likely we are to perceive it as relevant. Therefore, accuracy is way off. This is a consequence of our primal thoughts, and they are the enemy of higher thought processes. Social media perpetuates this with its magnification effect. In fact, a Twitter study confirms that false narratives travel six times farther and faster (Greenemeier, 2018) than truth, suggesting we need six interventions (accomplished through *stacking*) to overcome the falsehood.

No wonder school communities, and other organizations, face a hyperactive hive mindset, a manic groupthink. We are inundated with negative misinformation, and filtering through this can be complicated. The metrics online are engineered to mimic our habits, further convincing us of self-validating views, as in "See, I told you so!" While broadcasting facts out loud helps, how do we further unravel all of this in a way that produces a strong counterbalance?

It may seem obvious that the hyperactive hive mindset has become more prevalent in recent history as the world and our nation have faced a once-in-a-lifetime pandemic and growing concerns over equity. Violence and addiction trended upward, at sometimes alarming rates (Johnson, 2021). Building on recognition for these challenges allows radical leaders and their school community to tackle the dilemma with a conscious awareness, and to employ solutions to resolve them.

The Answer

Digesting all of this may have driven you to experience your own version of a hyperactive mindset. Rest easy. Radical Principals find unconventional solutions to these holistic challenges. Remember that lost in the fray of unresolved challenges are the most disadvantaged children. School communities can be a haven of safety for them. Yet students often have little power over the 16-18 hours each day that they live outside of school. Radical leaders must help teach them to escape the hyperactive hive mindset. How?

Students can learn to retreat to internal school influences that arm them against the frenzied world outside, in their community and on social media. Ironically, using each of these contexts is in some part, the way out of this complex and puzzling maze.

Therefore, radical efficiency inspires principals to implement two interconnected safety silos:

1. Sheltering learners and faculty for internal (in-school) opportunities to help them optimize use of their frontal lobe of higher thinking
2. Teaching one's school community about the external traps all are prone to and how to find escape hatches out.

<u>Internal Shelter</u>—no school is completely isolated and safe from the effects of the world outside. Yet the climate you commit to has a lasting impact on a child's experience. Arranging a school community with the structures that serve as a learning sanctuary can be one of the best ways to radically nurture the kind of focus that engages creative, frontal brain activity—the direct contrast to hyperactive minds. This is not something that happens automatically. These are carefully constructed with the kind of thoughtful management that allows schools to carve out a safe space for learning.

Many models of school systems that promote learner-friendly and safer environments may serve as exemplars. Some are commercialized, others are time-tested case studies which show how a school community remarkably redesigned for optimal teaching and learning, while using the school's own resources and time. New Jersey's Positive Behavior Support in Schools System (PBSIS), and the national program, Positive Behavior in Schools (PBIS) are examples.

PBSIS is a data-driven, tiered program of positive behavior tools to manage school climate issues, both at an individual, and a broader schoolwide level. The state department of education partners with Rutgers University/Robert Wood Johnson to provide training and assistance. A three-tiered intervention model for schools works to target supports for disadvantaged students (PBSIS, n.d.). The focus is on intervention, long-term solutions rather than short-term compliance, decreasing exclusion and discipline, and creating a new cycle of growth and acceptance, rather than conformity and containment.

School-wide positive learning models for all students are included in the pillars of success. Specific interventions for students with more intensive needs are integrated into the advanced components. Through the collaboration of the State Department of Education and Rutgers, the program has continued with noted influence since its founding in 2003. Research-based and evidence proven strategies are implemented in school communities.

Consider an example of a PBSIS-motivated program, and its influence on the school community. One school made hallways safer and saved eight school days of learning time. Getting students to class on time and clearing the halls can be difficult in many schools. The time between the established end of one class and the beginning of the next is often vaguely adhered to.

Students gather between classes to engage in social interactions. Class change times range from 2 to 5 minutes in schools and delays of student arrival to class are a persistent problem. The cost is lost time once classes have already begun, affecting everything from student learning, to time on task, to focus and schoolwide climate conditions. Frequently, students most in need of being in class and ready to learn are those not present, right when pivotal teaching and learning begins.

One principal was concerned by how delayed students arrival to their class was and how helpless teacher responses were that reinforced this. Teachers and administrators were unable to make timeliness to class a value that mattered to students. When students were in the halls, they were disrupting other classes, and disciplinary outcomes had little impact.

Imagine the level of disruptiveness to students who arrived to class ready, when a late arrival highlighted their lateness with a declaration of, "I'm here!," interrupting the flow of those ready to learn. The principal had learned about positive incentives that shift school climates, when properly implemented. He decided to try something new; a hall-by-hall team-based competitive format. He set out to shift negative punishment to positive opportunities

Ill-fated attempts for teachers to encourage students to comply caused an adverse effect, so why not try gaining student ownership? What better way to convince them than through some fun competition? A positive greeting by teachers inspires students to arrive ready and motivated (Allday & Pakurar, 2007), in significant, subtle ways that were worth the long term benefits.

The principal established the initiative by charting arrival times to determine a baseline. After one week of measuring the average time lost in the halls, in which he did not actively direct students to classes (a difficult but effective way to gather authentic data), he presented the results to his team to define school-wide goals.

The latency concern was abysmal with an average start time being 2.5 minutes *after* scheduled times. This was a substantial loss of instructional time for students. Measuring this time across a full 180 school day calendar meant eight school days were lost! See Appendix A for a minute-by-minute breakdown, useful for any school's own goal setting.

<u>There Was a Solution:</u> Since previous attempts at arrival timeliness failed, positive interventions were developed by instituting hall to hall races that were competitive and positive in nature. A hallway race was incorporated into the larger context of PBSIS. Students were awarded in winning hallways for getting to classrooms before others in the building and particularly, before the next class began.

<u>Outcome:</u> This became a terrific motivational tool to get students focused and engaged at the start of class, and arguably among the most prudent measures to get learning triggered. These races were conducted between classes at random moments throughout the day, at unannounced times. This allowed students and teachers an opportunity to motivate each other in their hallway during different stages and transitions of the day. There was a twofold result:

a. Learning engagement began faster and eliminated the disruptive patterns of onset to focus and accelerated learning time.
b. The hallways were cleared, reducing, or eliminating behavioral disruptions that resulted in a continuous cycle of negative behavior and removing ineffective ways to address them.

Winning hallways earned prize *tickets that were* entered into a lottery for each student and the teachers who issued them. This motivated the whole school community into a "You-win-I-win" mentality between students and the teachers, and classes working together to encourage everyone.

How It Changed the School: Students consistently arrived to class on time or within moments of the start, encouraged by the possibility that there could be a hall race, and the now-established expectation that they do not wander the halls. Teachers started earlier, avoided disruptions, and had less disturbances. Everyone bought into this win–win situation. The culture of the school changed, and students are in classrooms ready to learn. *Eight school days are saved*. That is a way to maximize learning and improve school climate.

This kind of comradery in competition can work in every school. While it is not a requirement that a positive behavior support program be in place to successfully employ this, it is helpful to adopt multiple approaches, to compound the effects of non-punitive interventions that are longer lasting. A list of positive behavior support interventions are found in Appendix B. The emphasis is on making it about "winning." Students and faculty are inspired by the competitive nature of the contest.

External Escape Hatches: Students are not in school for most of their day. During these times and spaces, educators have little control over what they are exposed to, and how to manage the many obstacles they encounter, especially regarding the inordinate amount of misinformation and negative content they are confronted with.

Children are connected to the digital world, more frequently indoors and sedentary. Encouraging and incentivizing them to get outside in nature is not just a great substitute for being online. Research shows that being in nature sharpens the mind (Weir, 2020). Outdoor exposure allows individuals to engage in more creative flow and thought processes, the antidote to digital distractions. Additionally, wellness is immediately shifted into a more encouraging direction when in harmony with nature, because doing so quite simply makes a person happier. Nature is part of our evolutionary wiring. People are connected to the outside world because they evolved in nature for millennia. This may seem obvious when you consider physiological nourishment from sources like Vitamin D from the Sun. Being inside most of the day reduces the Vitamin D our bodies need. Getting nourishment from Vitamin D is just one advantage to being outside, and it alone fights disease, depression and balances our body weight.

An evidence-based way to encourage children to be outside is to show them how doing so makes them happier, and more energized. This is reinforced by one's overall heightened state of wellness. The combination of detaching from media inside and replacing it with outdoor experiences is a strong combination that can enhance a student's motivation, energy, creativity, and overall, wellbeing.

Offering learners incentives to be outside and even for students to log their experience, for credit or for competition is a great starting point that can be used to motivate them. Offer them something of value so they can experience and learn to recognize all the benefits from nature.

Of course, outside options must always remain safe for children. Depending on the demographics of a child's location, we can offer outside alternatives at school, parks, public facilities, and other resources that provide a safe outdoor experience.

Since our responsibility does not end at the schoolhouse door, we can help students escape confusion and chaos in a world that can move too fast and furious for a highly focused mindset and state of wellbeing, simply by getting them outdoors.

Teaching children to incorporate self-regulation strategies helps them manage the ongoing distractions and alarming influx of social media news. This requires a strong commitment for us to teach them to understand the significance.

Radio Silence

It is important to highlight for families of students the distinctions between reliable evidence-based truths, valid resources, and the misinformation that permeates the social media landscape. Illustrating this for them, and the statistical probabilities highlighted previously can be a beneficial reinforcement for families.

Once the evidence is in and made clear, we can offer viable alternatives. The next step is to teach our students and families to substitute false narratives with fact-based practical solutions.

One way is to teach children to recognize the gravity of the effects caused by online misbehavior. Students do not readily realize the weight of consequences regarding their negative online conduct. These can be far-reaching. Colleges and employers have tools to examine historical online behavior through searchable, archived databases. Helping learners see that online misconduct is visible and reviewable to vet students can help them avoid the consequences before it is too late.

Additionally, we can help our learners see that negative social media interactions have an adverse effect on their body, mind, and overall wellness. In fact, it makes us less intelligent (Gaskell, 2021), which has long-term damaging effects on a student's aspirations and dreams, whatever they aspire to.

Using alternative offline tools, like ambient noise, journaling, and gratitude practices, offers antidotes to the detrimental effects associated with hyperactive mindsets that cause harmful impacts on children. These are useful tools to shift habit patterns. As Wood (2020b) explains, this results from a process within the application of implementing friction into routines.

We can add friction to counter unproductive habits, like removing our phone from next to our bed, to a location that makes it unreachable when resting. This reduces access to the continuous cycle of social media and other disruptions that keep distraction at a constantly heightened level of interference.

Removing bad habits by reducing friction is a good starting place to shift from ineffective groupthink toward group flow. It can be replaced by the habits we desire, something that allows users to establish as a consistently productive pattern, rather than the reverse. If you want to get up in the morning and exercise, put your workout clothes right next to your bed (where your phone used to be), so you can reduce friction, and grab them without much thought, or distraction.

The moment negative friction enters the picture (I have to dig my clothes out from under a pile of laundry), it slows us down and often, interferes with our good intention, with just enough distraction and difficulty to change our mind. Less friction automates the processes that are desirable, moving us toward functional behaviors because it requires less energy and thought to get there. Most methods that remove friction are simple and cumulative; we can add groups of them together to expand the effect of automating processes, and the fulfillment toward our desired goal.

Those often admired for great success do not have a magic wand or skills unobtainable to the rest of us. They do not possess some idealistic willpower that the average person cannot aspire to. Rather, they have established habits based on increasing friction where removal of bad habits is beneficial. Adding patterns of mind simplifies the steps to achieve an objective for them to avoid hesitation long enough to be focused on their best intentions.

Individuals like this have a whole inventory of systems in place and are consciously aware of making these shifts. This is the case with monumental milestones, and in common everyday practices alike. These subtle shifts are far more consequential when adjusted, due to building a steady upward momentum.

Consolidating an understanding of how disruptions evade the speed to be automatic in good practices with a framework helps students see the adverse and inaccurate effects of factors like toxic online behavior. Teaching them how to do this is not only a good idea, but it should be obligatory. Finally, radical efficiency is optimized when you enhance the likelihood of group flow, rather than a hyperactive hive mind, caused by the development of practices as simple and effective as manipulating friction in one's life.

Group flow cannot occur when a community is enduring a hyperactive hive mindset. Caught in a flurry of distracted confusion and misinformation, groupthink becomes counterproductive, illogical, and detrimental to the intended outcome. Group flow happens when the group hits that sweet spot of distraction-free, motivational, and creative solution-based collaboration.

This happens when teams come together, and organizations accomplish truly remarkable work, such as new innovations and ideas. Don't we owe it to our students, and families, to help them achieve their greatest, by having an additive multiplier effect to trigger those conditions? The multiplier effect works to nourish the efficiency of group flow because it generates an exponentially greater outcome than the original strategies. That is how something so remarkable as group flow achievements are realized.

Students and families should be taught the distinction between always being on and the solitude of a tranquil absence from digital disruption. Learning to harness this time in more constructive, higher-level ways yields incredibly productive results for individuals and groups, setting the stage for deep levels of work to occur. At the same time, this enables our families to remove compulsive and exhaustive behaviors that are counterproductive and unsatisfying, i.e. those unable to fulfill a never-ending urge of empty outcomes.

Summary

There are moments when outsourcing for productivity is not warranted. These are not as frequent as the moments when we should delegate menial tasks and work in ways that allow principals to engage in radical leadership. Principals efforts must focus on radical improvement, not the tedium of distraction. When you are drowning in bureaucracy, it is always better to beg for forgiveness, than to ask for permission.

Non-faculty personnel make up a significant portion of most schools and leveraging them as resources to help foster a radical school community is a superb way to create change agents for disadvantaged learners. Security personnel are excellent examples as they have grown in presence in schools and leveraging them to be assets as mentors to disadvantaged learners rather than antagonists to them is a surefire way to change a school culture for the better. The school effectively and efficiently reduces discipline, as suspension rates fall fast, and a school climate warms, offering a welcoming home for all.

One of the prime enemies of great, radical schools is the disinformation that prevails online, especially when it tricks us into thinking something is so much worse off, be it at a micro or macro level, then in reality it is. This is almost always the case and radical school leaders have a responsibility to change this within their schools. Confront this with strong rationale and teach facts to your entire school community. The awareness heuristic consolidates too much information, which produces an inaccurate, often misleading perception.

Internal (within-school) and external strategies taught to students can help them manage the onslaught of misinformation and fear and turn them instead toward higher-level thought processes. Positive behavior support programs offer promising interventions that work to support school communities and their disadvantaged learners.

Basic techniques, like changing hallway behavior, can positively result in students being ready to learn and focused. External escapes away from school include being in nature because research shows how being in nature sharpens the mind. Vitamin D is just one aspect of the value of being outside, and it alone fights disease, depression and balances our body weight.

Teaching children that the consequences of their online conduct are far-reaching and may directly affect their future goals can act as a deterrent. Helping students understand that these online disruptions are also destructive in a physiological and cognitive sense can further deter their negative conduct online. Using alternative strategies to help quiet and focus the mind can reverse these effects.

Friction is a method to eliminate bad habits and automate positive new ones. Engaging in friction, we can ease the transition to good habits (exercise clothes next to our bed so we work out) and avoid bad habits (phone next to bed is too close to be distracted). The stream of upturns begins to catalyze broader and more accelerated achievements. Understanding this momentum and using it to move forward rather than backward in progress is highly relevant to the learner. The multiplier effect works to nourish group flow efficiency because it generates a compound effect that is exponentially greater than the original separate contributions. Changing from negative, toxic online disruptions to individual and group flow is the way forward for optimal productivity and wellness.

5

Radical Communication = Radical *Change*

Principals face intrusions that bombard them which can quickly overwhelm leaders and disrupt their best intentions. As discussed in the previous chapter, one of these disruptions is digital communication. This can be an interruption that impairs a Radical Principal's best intentions. School leaders receive messages that are tediously long, may contain an important point or two, lost in a diatribe of minutiae, and takes too much time to dissect relevant context from.

Quickly, principals become overwhelmed by lengthy, excessive messages, bound to deciphering the meaning of the content, much or all of which warrants a response. Excessive and unproductive back-and-forth exchanges that instigate misunderstanding, frustration, and confusion abound. Educators have all endured these exasperating exchanges in our digital lives (Baer, 2016; Shukle, 2015).

This is wasteful, and there are solutions to overcome these exchanges so that we can return to the important work of helping children. Doing so enables principals to spend more time and

DOI: 10.4324/9781003275718-5

resources being radically creative, rather than caught up in distracting and escalating exchanges.

First, differentiate messages that are urgent; these are few, from those that can be dealt with later, these are many. An example of an urgent message is when a threat is posed to a student or staff member. Perhaps word is received that a child is in danger because others are planning to harm them with violence. This requires leaders to drop everything and act.

More commonplace in a principal's day, is when someone has a question, or seeks clarification on something far less consequential. These may be presented as urgent by the person, but almost never are, and should not be reacted to with matching urgency. Otherwise, leaders will react all day, and never get to the real radical work in supporting children. They also fail in modeling important management to their school community. Reactionary leadership further leads to poorer processing and decision-making. Consider, would you rather wander through the trivialities of the day or make radical progress?

Establish the expectation that although everyone's concern is important (at least to them), it will be addressed in a reasonable, though not immediate fashion. This must remain uncompromising.

Build Distraction-Free Zones to Enhance Radical Communication

School leaders gain from building protective factors in their day to prevent low-level work, such as sifting through their email first thing in the morning, when optimal opportunities should be harnessed. Assuming it is efficient, they may feel pressured, presenting a false sense of accomplishment, when almost nothing is truly gained.

Sorting through email exchanges causes principals to start their day with a reactive mindset that reinforces an instinctively lower gear, distant from our true goal: to trigger higher-level thinking. These are exceptional, ingenious, and break away moments to seize on. It is easy to be lulled into the desire to satisfy the mundane, to finish our digital messaging, to conquer that inbox. Yet it is the wrong path when we can instead prime our minds for next level success to advance school communities in broader contexts.

Like a checklist, many of us feel as though we must cross off each message, just as individuals are compelled to scroll through their social media feed and reach for their phone at the start of their day. Impulses act to satisfy a quick hit in our always-on mentality, a false sense of security that conspires to drag us into a deceptive sense of satisfaction and ultimately, toward reactive management. Proactive leadership is inhibited.

This drags school leaders into an endless pit of questions and answers, often a never-ending feedback loop. Email exchanges spiral further out of control. Radical leaders recognize this and redirect message retrieval and response duties into other portions of their day when they are less likely to hinder their focus, their time to be radical. For instance, earlier it was mentioned how late afternoon is a low-energy and creativity cycle for most, which results in lower-level cognition. Use low-level cycles for tasks like responding to emails and preserve those high-energy, high-focus moments for radical action

The secondary benefit of waiting out messages until later is that, oftentimes, those inquiring have resolved their own issues and you get the follow-up message before you have a chance to respond: "Never mind, I/we figured it out!" The added benefit to this is that it allows individuals to process information before responding, encouraging them to problem-solve on their own. The skill becomes reinforced, never mind the subtraction of micromanagement.

This is a tremendous way to encourage those in your school community to come up with ideas, both empowering for themselves, and without burdening you nonstop for answers to common problems. In and of itself, this promotes an instrumental culture shift that rewards the school community through learning.

Since it is typical for principals to encounter ever-intensifying messages from various members of the school community, a principal risks being pulled away from more focused, productive, and better-grounded work. Most of us at one time or another have been lulled into *email* or *social media wars*: an endless exchange of back-and-forth that pries us away from our innovative efforts to develop opportunities for student gain. Keyboard warriors (Eitner, 2019) work to manipulate you from behind a computer screen, and this can cause destruction in the path of the Radical Principal.

These are healthy for no one, none of the time. In fact, a University of Buffalo study (2018) showed how negative messaging reduces cognitive processes to a lower level, putting us in a more primal state. We literally become less intelligent! That is bad news for those who wish to make radical changes in schools, and the kids counting on their school leaders to do so.

A rule provided by Jay Baer (2016) regarding customer service is well worth using for radical school communication. *Reply only twice*, in conquering the keyboard warriors (Eitner, 2019). This concept is based on broader customer service principles and how our emotions interfere with productive management from intensified attacks online. Applying this principle to school communities presents a prescriptive response technique that addresses ongoing and counterproductive back-and-forth exchanges, allowing us to redirect our energy where it counts.

Reply Only Twice(How It Works)

A customer (school community member) reaches out, expressing dissatisfaction with a service, staff member or resource. The agent responding attempts to remedy the situation. The customer pushes back with an ever-escalating response. How does the agent respond?

According to Baer (2016), always acknowledge and apologize, even if their reaction is disproportionate to the issue, or flat out wrong. Acknowledgement often settles an unsatisfied individual and gets them back on a resolution oriented track with you. If the customer remains antagonistic, with an aggressive reaction that begins something like, "no, I REALLY hate…" answer a second time and offer a solution or alternative communication means (phone, meeting, etc.). Get them offline and provide options.

If they reply a third time, doubling down with unreasonable demands and tension, do not get consumed with their negative feedback loop. You seek resolution, but the more important element of online communications are the bystanders, those on the sidelines witnessing, hearing about, or affected by these exchanges. Remember always that children are affected, somewhere squarely in the mix.

Once you are on record as listening and attempting to solve the issue, you have documented that you are reasonable and seeking resolution in a thoughtful way. Engaging in an eye-for-an-eye approach anywhere online is always counterproductive for everyone. This is especially the case for Radical Principals, as they get pulled away from innovative opportunities. This is, at the very least, an unproductive distraction that degrades positive energy as educators anxiously and defensively anticipate the next set of heightened exchanges.

Model appropriate behavior in these forums. Always assume that every message you write will be posted online, everywhere. If all your efforts are focused on offering solutions and the person on the other end is increasing the tension, it is reasonable to cease correspondence. If the person wishes to return to a resolution later, and tempers their response, open the door wide. Always be ready for resolution, but with civil and clear standards, that are modeled for students and adults alike.

Often in the context of schools, a parent, or other community member, is our unsatisfied customer. The problem may be related to a child or communication with a member of your staff. The scenario begins with a livid email from the parent toward the teacher, you, or both. The common mistake is for the recipient to react defensively. This only reinforces the person's perception that warrants your feeling compelled to be defensive.

In exchanges like these, it is more effective to express your regret at their dissatisfaction and offer a time to talk. If the parent responds in an emotionally charged way, using Baer's (2016) approach, the educator delivers the expectation and willingness that the conversation should go offline, for a more interactive and direct attempt to resolve the issue.

Verbal interactions are far more effective since a great deal of misunderstanding so often underlies online correspondences. These misunderstandings are rooted in assumptions that can be easily and accurately clarified once our intent is made clear with a pleasant, approachable tone. We demonstrate care and responsiveness, as opposed to the appearance of sarcasm or coldness, often perpetuated online.

This approach is also far less time-consuming, an ironic twist for busy educators who may make the costly assumption that electronic communication is more efficient, quicker, and easier. This is because of how people are inclined to seek information. Distinguishing between these helps the leader to define how to respond:

a) objective, which is factual.
b) subjective, which offers more of an opinion.

Let us consider how to respond in each circumstance.

Objective content is fact-based and allows information to flow more accurately in email, posts, and chat responses. An example of objective messaging is, "What sections will the test be on?" Our reply is specific, and therefore bears minimal error in translating, reducing misinformation or misinterpretation. "The test will be on sections 3.4 and 3.5, review your notes. Good luck!"

Note the pleasantry at the end. This is helpful when the request is testy or impolite. We always maintain and model professional and courteous conduct. Thus, objective responses are straightforward, matter-of-fact and courteous. This allows a reference point later if needed when calling out a repeatedly insulting person on the other end. It becomes even more significant when engaging in subjective dialogue.

Subjective context frequently involves the circumstance to employ the reply only twice method; a more direct approach using verbal dialogue. When questions or suggestions of a subjective nature arise, avoid written responses at all costs.

Consider, for instance, a child who misbehaved in class and was directed to *sit down and be quiet*. He returns home, only to report to his parents that he was *doing nothing wrong*, and his teacher told him to *shut up and sit down*! An emotionally charged email awaits the teacher: *How dare you, how could you talk to my child like that. Who do you think you are?!?* In one exchange, the blame has shifted.

Distressed at the misrepresentation of facts, the teacher often feels compelled to launch into a detailed, defensive posture. This almost always brings about a response by the parent which intensifies the tension rather than calming them down. *Are you calling my child a liar?* By calling or writing a tempered response to request an opportunity to speak, the teacher can redirect the anger toward constructive dialogue, with thoughtfully placed intonation.

This happens because when writing responses, we appear on the other side as a two-dimensional avatar. It is easy to assume the worst about a robotic, inhumane characterization. When we represent ourselves through direct verbal dialogue, we are shifting a person's view of us, to our more authentic three-dimensional self, with thoughts, feelings and care for their child. We are human. This approach far outpaces written attempts.

Endlessly laboring over two-dimensional, demonizing written responses, gets educators sucked in and as bad, we view the other person in the same destructive way.

By engaging in direct dialogue with our school community members, we model this expectation for our faculty too. We establish the expectation that seeking direct dialogue is the best approach, part of our process as a school, and that it effectively reduces misunderstanding, while shifting toward relationship building. All faculty must regularly practice this approach. This is especially true when we employ the standard of *replying only twice*.

Messaging: If You Cannot Go Through, Go Around

Tom Bilyeu (2021), successful entrepreneur and creator of Quest Bars, characterized the willingness to operate within and around the rules as putting your ego aside to achieve something greater (radical):

> When you understand how the game works, and you don't demand that the world act as if you wish it does, you can now win because you're not fighting yourself or "the man".
>
> (Tom Bilyeu, June 29, 2021, 19:25)

Principals serve in the role of problem solver. They are accustomed to troubleshooting many day-to-day challenges. They are often confronted suddenly with issues that their school community counts on them to resolve. Sometimes, that resolution is just to listen. At other times, it is more.

As middle managers, principals frequently find themselves positioned between opposing views and this can create real dilemmas. Imagine that on one side, you have an individual who is expecting a satisfactory conclusion, that is from their point of view. On the other side, there is a strongly opposing perspective and a contradicting set of values for how to address the same issue.

The problem with these all-too-common situations is that when a school leader is wedged in between, it can make the principal appear as though he is indecisive and unable to enact constructive change from the middle. This is certainly a more significant conflict when it limits the kind of results that should serve to benefit students. On these occasions, principals must learn to shift away from going through with a message to going around. Let us examine how and why this works far more effectively in given circumstances.

The Bully on the Bus

One of the most problematic issues in schools is when political pressure stands in the way of helping a victimized child. Phil was such a child: kind, softly spoken, introverted and small. A peer had been teasing him on the bus, with increasing intensity for months. Discipline was issued and interventions instituted each time. Yet the bully on the bus kept seeking this child out and targeting Phil more intensely. Short-term bus suspensions had no impact on his behavior. He continued to intimidate, insult, and demean little Phil.

This persistent problem was reinforced by the aggressor's parents who challenged the school's authority while ignoring their child's behavior. The victim had been bullied yet again, as he was blocked while trying to get to his bus seat, was cursed at, and faced increasingly intimidating behavior. Phil's dad pleaded with the school's administration. *Can't you stop the bullying?!?* Compelled to act, the principal had to issue an ultimatum.

With three months still remaining in the school year, the principal met with the offender's parents and warned that if their son bullied Phil again, he would be removed from the bus, permanently for the remainder of the year. In spite of this warning, the child targeted Phil again, perpetrating a hostile situation as he repeatedly refused to let Phil pass by to his seat, and shouted names at him while the bus was in motion.

The principal followed through and alerted the offender's parents that their son was permanently removed from the bus. They threatened the principal with legal action, and charged over to his superior's office, to complain. Moments later, his supervisor contacted him, insisting that this child be immediately reinstated to the bus.

Several futile attempts to implore the supervisor went unchecked. Having documented the incident officially, the principal had clearly agitated his superior. With the concern officially memorialized, this student could not return to the bus. With an irritated tone, his superior demanded the principal *get the child on another bus and call the parent back to explain the resolution*!

The principal worried that the aggressor would move on to another vulnerable child on his new bus, and, again, would not be held accountable. A terrible message was being sent about the school (and principal's perceived) inaction. One can imagine how demoralizing this experience must have felt for our school leader. His authority had been stripped from him, not due to an error on his part, but rather as the result of some senseless unknown political motive.

The principal contacted the supervisor of transportation to discuss how to reinstate the aggressor on another bus. If the events stopped here, it would regrettably be like so many that force principals in the middle into unsettling decisions, the kind that keep them up at night. The supervisor found the closest bus route and noted that there was a problem. The bus travels in the opposite direction and this student's street is one mile long. The bus can only drop him off at the end of the road because it is a dead end. The turn cannot be made that way.

The principal knew he was within his legal right to proceed with this: many students had safely walked home from greater distances. He replied, *I don't see a problem with that, do you see a problem with that?* The transportation supervisor paused for a moment, and then caught on, straightening up in her seat and stating, oh, *no I don't see a problem with that either!*

Next, the principal contacted the parent of the offending student, to inform them about the bus reassignment. A couple of days later, he received a call back from the parent who asked, *did you know that the new bus drops my son off a mile from our house?*

When justice prevails, it is moments like these that offer a leader the satisfaction to let it all sink in. His response was quite simply, *Really?* The parent responded, *yes, it is ... I think I'm going to drive him to school for the rest of the year.* The principal remained cordial, and careful not to sound sarcastic in any way and replied, *I think that's a good idea.*

Knowing when to step aside and allow unexpected forces to take over in the place of the principal to solve a problem is a strategy that resulted in an objective being met, something that has the potential to occur far more frequently than leaders might expect. Recognizing the difficulty of pushing directly against rigidly opposing forces like the politically motivated central office administrator demonstrated how little control principals in the middle often have, and how they can leverage unexpected methods to achieve their desired outcome anyway.

> When you understand how the game works, and you don't demand that the world act as if you wish it does, you can now win because you're not fighting yourself or "the man."
>
> (Tom Bilyeu, June 29, 2021, 19:25)

It would seem outrageous that political pressure overrides ethical support for a marginalized child. It happens far more often than educators would like to admit. There are times when playing out the circumstances, riding the momentum of an unexpected turn of events, allows radical leaders to follow a path of justice served to the benefit of a disadvantaged child.

How this was accomplished mattered far less than that it was. The principal put his pride aside long enough to let the storm ride out and, in the end, a child got to ride his bus safely. Justice prevailed, even as the route toward it seemed unexpected. This all-too-common scenario exists in the political landscape of schools. Many are influenced by pressures that override objective and ethical decision-making. Understanding this and not pushing back against political forces helped this principal realize the solution can often come from an unexpected angle.

Protecting Children from Toxic Bureaucracy

Methods for working through and around gridlock caused by poorly managed governance of schools provokes Radical Principals to seek out long-term resolution, rather than short-term, temporary satisfaction. Remember that the end goal is not how outcomes are achieved but rather that they are and, what benefits students gain from our influence, regardless of the approach. When bureaucracy stands in the way, Radical Principals become creative, or they let others do the work for them. Another example of working around rather than through a dilemma follows.

Tragedy strikes communities, and, in schools, hits everyone harder when children are involved. In one school, a child tragically drowned over a weekend, and the community grieved this devastating loss. Upon returning to school, a student unfamiliar with this child, or the nuances of families grieving his loss, wondered out loud, on social media, why *everyone seemed to be making such a big deal out of this…*

This child lacked a true sense of the tragedy and pain resulting from the loss of a child, and particularly how this impacted others in the school community. Word traveled fast to school officials that the child who posted the comment had enraged students close to the lost child. They were seeking revenge. They planned to assault this child at their first opportunity, in the hall during school.

Seeing a clear and present danger, the principal mobilized his school security team, discussed the issue, and detailed which classrooms and times the student would be traveling between over the course of his school day. He requested they keep a close eye on the student during passing time. Be sure to watch his entry, route, and exit, he explained. Behind the scenes, his administration was busy fielding the challenges brought on by emotional escalation among the families and students.

The security officers responded that they were not permitted to *escort children around the building*. Feeling pressured by the moment, the principal looked at the clock, alerted security that this was an urgent matter, and that he needed them to closely monitor the child's movements. The security officer repeated that this was *direct supervision*, and they were not permitted to fulfill his request. The principal, in frustration, directed his security to follow his directive. He instructed that this would be addressed later with clarification, with the supervisor of security.

With reluctance, the security officer complied and, fortunately, the child remained unharmed that day. Armed with time to manage the crisis, counseling intervention shifted from potential violence to conflict resolution. Yet this raised a larger concern. How could security question a direct request from the building principal, especially while the clock was ticking in a potentially hazardous situation, affecting the security and safety of children?

Anticipating certain agreement, the principal shared his concern with the head of security expecting that there would be a simple consensus. Yet when presented, he was alarmed to learn that the director disagreed and resisted endorsing the principal. Exasperated, the principal wondered: how could any staff member, regardless of rank or position, refuse to protect the safety of any child under such urgent circumstances?

As word spread of this, and additional refusals by security about *direct student supervision* ensued, the school's faculty representatives requested this be brought up at a district level.

Here, an outlet heard by superiors in central office may have a better outcome than what had been unsuccessfully attempted at the building level.

While the supervisor of security had rejected the principal's initial appeal, it was in this context, in a more public and official forum, that a concession was made. The supervisor agreed that student safety had to come before job descriptions. Members representing the faculty had successfully accomplished what the principal was unable to and in the end, children in the school were safer as a result of their more formal appeal.

The principal had been made aware by faculty that they were moving forward with the formal complaint. He did not know what to expect. Yet being radical sometimes means taking a step back and letting others leap in to be agents of change. Power down so others can power up. The outcome? The principal can call on his security team, as well as other assigned personnel to monitor and protect the welfare of children. Stepping back from one's leadership role can be radical when the outcome is fulfilled. Mission accomplished.

These two scenarios: the bully on the bus and the security supervision issue were examples of goals that can be accomplished in radically, unusual, and even indirect ways. If they serve to benefit students, the way in which the goal was accomplished does not matter. All children gain when a principal knows to take a radical step back at times when it helps, rather than forward, when it hinders.

Imperfect is More Effective than Flawless Customer Service

Businesses spend a tremendous amount of time and resources working on customer satisfaction. In the online world of ratings lifelines, organizations must be sharply focused on how they are perceived by their customers and actively monitor this status. There has been increased acceptance in schools on the value of treating families as satisfied customers too.

Yet school communities often overlook the degree of importance customer service has for customers (their families). This bears tremendous cost because not feeling valued causes damage to the school's long-term reputation, and it takes more energy to unravel, after a problem has been left unresolved or delayed too long.

Radical communication involves increased appreciation for how customer service attunes school to the way they are perceived. School branding has become popular in education blogs (West-Rosenthal, 2020) and there is growing recognition of a school's perceptions by their community. Within the limited literature base reinforcing this is an emphasis on schools to present a premium public appearance. Make sure everything looks wonderful on the surface. Yet schools should instead aim for a dynamic, well-connected, responsive, and trusting, if not imperfect way to service their families.

Beyond appearance is the recognition that the most successful brands and organizations shift past presentation and packaging and look deeper, recognizing their own imperfections. They cleverly use errors to their *advantage*. These organizations reap benefits from a formula that produces considerable favor, rather than reacting when it's too late, with foot-dragging resistance that results in falling out of favor.

Consider consumers when contemplating this: they are well versed in identifying effectively-run organizations. People are imperfect, fallible human beings and customers know this and the potential for human error. Schools are also places of learning, and, as such, can promote the imperfect learning curve all productive individuals, and organizations experience in their own path growth and success.

The difference for successful organizations, especially those that are people-minded businesses such as schools, is that these organizations identify, and embrace their mistakes. They work hard to rectify errors, reinforcing customer satisfaction, in a timely and responsive manner. They are transparent about not running flawlessly. That artificial pretense only gets organizations and individuals as far as face value. So, what do organizations (and people) do to acknowledge their imperfections and gain the loyalty of others at the same time?

Timeliness and *responsiveness* are the chief components to bring a sense of satisfaction to our families (the customer). Response time to customers is crucial. When this occurs in schools, families feel attended to. A critical element is that they are not feeling as though they are being ignored. This is an invaluable response structure to adhere to because there is perhaps no worse perception than organizations who appear to ignore their customer concerns. Added to this is that customers have the leverage to make this known, publicly online, with their social media megaphone.

Whether a lack of responsiveness is intentional or not, lackluster follow-through conveys that those operating within the organizational framework simply do not care. That is bad business in any organization, arguably even worse in schools, where children are involved. Responding in a timely manner allows families the satisfaction of knowing that they have been heard and that there will be a sincere attempt at resolution.

Responsiveness is the second element in this strategic approach. Being responsive shows a genuine dedication to resolution. Customers do not necessarily expect to be provided with a perfect response, they just want the issue corrected, and an acknowledgement that a mistake was made. Of course, there are exceptions to this, as addressed earlier when responding to unreasonable demands online (Baer, 2016). Remember the rule to reply only twice in these instances.

Most individuals find tremendous satisfaction in a *timely* and *responsive* approach. In fact, customers report greater appreciation with organizations who approach corrections in this way, versus those who never fielded a complaint in the first place (Weiche, 2016). One study revealed the too good to be true perception by customers, such as five-star reviews are met with skepticism.

A more trusted set of ratings falls between 4.2 and 4.5—strong, yet humanly imperfect (Collinger, 2016).

It is profound to consider that customers demonstrate greater loyalty to an organization that is responsive to an issue over an error-free one. This is due to a fundamental psychology: individuals appreciate the effort to correct something more than when they experience perfect service. Shukle (2015) considers how companies can meet with much success in employing a correction-based approach, rather than trying to be unrealistically error free.

Making mistakes provides a path to improvement which results in tremendous customer devotion to such an extent that commitment increases when experiencing this kind of response. Schools can learn from this when managing issues with families and their school community. It is acceptable to apologize and start over, something that seems to be avoided ad nauseum by less radical leaders. Perhaps this is for fear of being judged or the worry that detrimental consequences will result. That is an ironic twist when Radical Principals know that a remedy brings about the kind of respect and loyalty that overtakes unreachable perfect service.

Steps to resolution: One of the most challenging parts of achieving satisfaction relates to timeliness of response. This can cause conflict when we struggle to manage our efforts to address conflicts with time and energy. How do we balance timeliness of response with our commitment to working through the complex nuances of a problem?

Recall that most decisions do not necessitate an urgent resolution. Actions can be delayed long enough to get answers. One principal encountered a parent calling and demanding a response within ten minutes or he would call the superintendent's office. Yet the principal was observing a class and could not abandon his pre-arranged obligation. Additionally, his office staff knew enough about the issue that this was not an urgent matter. It could wait. He asked his secretary to call back with the following message:

> Your concern is important to me, and therefore, I do not want to respond pre-maturely, without gathering the necessary information to make a careful and thought-out determination. I cannot fairly do so without first giving you the time and attention you deserve. Would you please give me the opportunity to follow up on this matter and respond, so we can work together to resolve the issue?

Note that this request for more time includes key elements that put timing back in control of the principal while at the same time offering to acknowledge the parent's concern. The school leader is affirming that this issue is clearly of value to the complainant and that it will be addressed. It is for this reason that the administrator is justified in calling for more time.

Appealing to your customer base with a request to take the time to investigate an issue buys time, and few, if any individual seeking a response can debate this logic. Additionally, a Radical Principal can examine the issue behind the scenes, so that important background information is gathered, and a fuller understanding of the issue comes into focus. This helps prepare the leader when speaking with the concerned parent in this context.

Requests for a time extension can also be communicated electronically if the person prefers this context or is unavailable by phone. There is nothing in this messaging that a principal could fear to be twisted, taken out of context, forwarded, or planted on a social media feed for others to see. It is defensible in any context, even admirable, because of the rationale provided and commitment to follow up. Rationalizing a thorough and unrushed response demonstrates care and commitment to a response, while redirecting unreasonable "act-now" demands.

Keep in mind that like other radical methods, most of these ideas work, most of the time. There is no panacea, no cure-all. Rather, radical leaders are aiming for ways to address challenges which make their work more pragmatic in supporting student success. They consider context and options. Having a set of pre-established practices allows Radical Principals to try, and try again, until success is reached. Understanding this liberates school leaders from the end-alls they are mistakenly pressured into regarding as their work.

Summary

One of the burdens of school leaders is the large quantity of digital exchanges that paralyze their best intentions. Attempting to resolve a back-and-forth exchange can cause the reverse, with escalating exchanges, resulting from misunderstanding. The digital disruptions that interrupt a principal's day must be prioritized. Most of these are not urgent and should be addressed later. Only truly critical issues can be allowed to interrupt a Radical Principal's progress.

Understanding the moments in a school leader's day that are primed for higher-level ingenuity and then protecting times to grant these moments is imperative. Understanding when low-level times in the day are, we can address lower-level and mundane tasks in these moments. Also, giving people the time to process their problem often enables them to think through and solve it before you arrive at their dilemma. Teaching them to do this in an invaluable solution that subtracts from your load.

Reply only twice allows school leaders to radically define their willingness to respond and hold moral ground in the process. It satisfies the need to be approachable, yet focused. In these circumstances, always be ready for resolution, but with civil and clear standards. Breaking down digital communications and understanding how to address these is instrumental in the way we both deescalate and stand our ground in responding to issues. Most often, get the conversation offline. Making a more direct appeal humanizes us to the person, and more clearly addresses the concern.

It is fairly safe to communicate digitally about factual, objective information. Subjective, emotionally connected contexts should be moved offline. Understanding this distinction will help prioritize how to communicate. Always seek offline, direct dialogue. Endlessly laboring over two-dimensional, demonizing written responses, we get sucked in and view them in the same destructive way.

Being radical means not fighting yourself, or a larger force, but, often, working around those forces to achieve your objective. Recognizing injustices, like a bully on a bus whose parents (ironically) bullied their way over the principal to keep their student on the bus, often mandates the principal take a step back, and let other forces drive justice. Letting others do the work for us is not easy for Radical Principals; at times, however, it is the most effective route around bureaucracy. A similar approach works when building-level decisions are unreasonably obstructed, and those with seemingly less authority can invoke the change. Being radical sometimes means taking a step back and letting others leap in to be agents of change.

Providing families with imperfect, yet responsive customer service breeds a stronger connection with them than error-free, or unresponsive service. Making mistakes provides a path to progress and improvement, which results in tremendous customer devotion so much so that commitment increases when experiencing this kind of response.

Use radical communication to aim for the adaptable space that offers ways to address challenges that make our work more pragmatic in supporting student success.

6

Radical Networking

Principals often operate in isolated silos. It is imperative to understand the challenges of seclusion, to limited reference points or guides to thoughtfully manage the unavoidable and inevitable problems that test school leaders. Charting this course alone is overwhelming, daunting and unhealthy for the leader's wellbeing. This is not beneficial for a person of such influence, especially when they impact children who need their support in such profound ways.

The way to navigate through these difficulties is anchored in safe spaces to check a leader's fears, worries and concerns. This can be accomplished through a networking support approach. Coaching and mentoring programs have become increasingly prevalent outlets for organizational leaders in a variety of professions. Progress for access to coaching and mentoring in educational leadership contexts has been slower-moving. Yet it is at least as warranted, if not more when working with children, and especially navigating the challenges of aiding children in the greatest need.

DOI: 10.4324/9781003275718-6

Coaching and mentoring programs are invaluable tools for leaders because they work so well when the efforts behind purposeful relationship building, and investments in time and resources are better allocated. What is crucial for principals is to forge a path to connect with colleagues, an access point which is uncomplicated, attainable and resourceful. Programs like this exist. Mastermind groups are one professional access point. In very different organized groups, with programs of recovery, like 12-step programs, these safe havens for networking support also exist.

It may seem quite unusual to relate educational leadership support networks to programs of recovery, and it certainly is. Otherwise, it would not be radical. Let us take a closer look at why masterminds and programs of recovery radically concep-tualize benefits translating how similar models of support can aid school leaders in need of the bonds developed in organized mastermind-formatted groups.

A significant factor in why mastermind and recovery pro-grams have worked to help hundreds of thousand, or more individuals, in needed circumstances, as a tool, a shoulder to lean on is that they provide a structured, built-in community support framework. This network functions with a common language, just as principals share in their building leadership needs when they connect in similarly coordinated ways.

Support programs do not happen alone or in a single, land-mark moment. They are an ongoing journey that take a whole community, working together along the way. A common bond of like-minded individuals has the capacity to create a robust and thriving network. Mastermind and recovery programs help individuals manage their challenges, by removing the problems associated with destructive isolation. These programs provide a shared and secure social professional network with others who share common goals and experiences along their journey. This may be in recovery, or in the case of principals, in their professional development and growth process.

Leadership coaches are trained to guide individuals, steering them toward opportunities for success. If properly executed and sourced, coaching models are invaluable resource programs. The challenge with coaching models is that they typically require considerable financial obligations, which may not be readily accessible, especially in organizations with more limited resources. Ironically, they may also be less supported in lower economically supported school communities, where they are most needed.

More impoverished school communities are primarily identified as being in the most-needed support networks. Life and corporate coaches have grown in demand and popularity because they work quite well when properly instituted. Yet coaches do not provide their service for free. While coaching programs can and do serve a valuable purpose in supporting school leaders, they are not always accessible as long term and viable support networks that can continue past a grant funded project or given initiatives. To work, these kinds of programs must be provided without such limitations of time and access

What differentiates radical networks is how groups of principals, from across states and nations, find a safe harbor within support programs. They allow school leaders to connect, where their creativity can flow, ideas can be shared, and guidance and encouragement can be provided in a judgment-free zone. Frustrations can be vented, all in an agreed-upon safe space at low or no cost. Even school leaders within a district or region face the political pressures that may forge natural trust barriers. They need an outlet, a place to go where colleagues not engaged in the same political structures can work with each other to help achieve a common goal in striving for radical leadership.

Colleagues working closely together bear the costs of accountability within the same organization. Close contacts inside organizations reduce the ease with which radical networking programs can operate without fear of reprisal, either true or perceived. Radical Principal Networks, just like mastermind and recovery groups, can liberate principals from this fear, and allow them to authentically and pragmatically express their frustrations, desires, ideals, and common interests This occurs in mobilized contexts that allow leaders to engage in innovative, judgement free zones.

Like masterminds and recovery programs, radical networks mobilize relationships and bonds in the shelter of connected webs across school and geographic spaces. They exist in digital form, in-person, county, and regionally coordinated groups, and in hybrid networks of both digital and in-person contexts. Radical networks allow principals to be freed from the constraints of political restrictions that permeate organizational governance within and across school communities. This provides a significant catalyst to empower principals to experience the freedom from inhibiting consequences as a sanctuary of safety within their networks.

Mastermind, coaching, and support groups have a commonality in the connection of bonds existing between persons with a common interest. They actively promote the benefits of wellness in their support of individuals. A heavy emphasis on wellness includes mindful engagement, through practiced methods. These may include methods like arranging planned opportunities for contemplation and meditation. Practicing these important self-care techniques in the group further reinforces the freedom for school leaders to become more radically effective.

Though not an all-inclusive list, some of the highlights of self-care practices in groups are presented. A prevailing amount of evidence exists about why meditation for one, is so helpful, in support networks and life to help individuals perform at more optimal levels, individually and within groups. Consider why meditation provides such valuable advantages for those who practice it within the constraints and demands they face. Mindful practices engage individuals in a much deeper thought process within the brain: tapping into those parts that relate to higher degrees of cognition- the mid-front and back portions.

Evidence on magnetic resonance imaging (MRI) shows how considerably increased activity occurs in areas of the brain that stimulate reasoning. These parts of the brain provide for the nurturance of self-reflection and self-regulation mechanisms. Tuning these areas with targeted focus results in an ideal balance of both high cognition and calming techniques. This balance is an effective sweet spot for radical leaders to pursue. These balance points are the phases that can be maximized, and they stimulate the potential for radical thinking in leadership practices.

Consider the impact. Research suggests meditation practices reduce cravings, so substantially, that long-term growth and treatment has drastically altered the trajectory of many individuals lives. This has had such a profound impact on so many individuals, that studies show how they have been able to live long, productive lives as a result of the intermittent practice of meditation (Thorpe, 2020).

This, along with the evidence that meditation can literally rewire the structure of a person's brain, is a primary reason that fight or flight reactions, which normally override the possibility for frontal brain thoughts, cannot mask the ingenuity brought on by meditation. More sophisticated, logical functioning replaces primal thought processes during and beyond the meditation practice.

In other words, the effects of meditation continue long after applying the technique. They do not just benefit a person during the practice. The effects of mindful exercises keep going, long after the actual practice has surpassed. That is radical. Remarkably, just 20 minutes of meditation allows a person's body to rest so deeply, that this degree of relaxation is double the effect of the soundest sleep (Thompson, 2021). This may persuade those who argue that they do not have time for it. Twenty minutes of proper guidance provides a far larger output of impact.

Meditation does not have to be the only focus-inducing and wellness practice employed, in mastermind groups, or individually. Other techniques are outlined in this text, including more accessible ways for a person to retrieve strategies right within their present work environment. These include concepts provided in greater detail later, such as targeted background noise, and tuning the brain's auditory senses in focused ways that trigger specific physiological and mindful reactions.

By applying practices of meditation and providing connections to others with common bonds in safe zones, the benefits for those implementing a radical networking program are virtually unlimited. For as long as educational leaders have been operating school communities, they have informally practiced within established specialized, if not informal frameworks. Mobilizing, formalizing, and expanding these in structured, cohesive ways, yields even stronger, more consistent, and sustainable results for educators to employ for a greater mind–body connection, entitling the leader to give back to her school community in far greater ways.

Enlist Radical Principal Networks. Create opportunities that allow individuals to practice mindful techniques together and to learn skills from each other. Develop methods for higher states of flow, in a safe, more liberating context. It may be simpler to connect with groups like this, through social media, and can also include attendance at conferences at regional, state, and national levels.

Groups from Facebook, Twitter, YouTube, and conferencing apps can quickly allow school leaders to assemble mastermind types of networks in convenient ways. For the school leader who desires next-level success, they gain the kind of benefits for students that are longer lasting and more profound. It is for these reasons that masterminds and the practices within them offer an attractive pursuit for Radical Principals.

Summary

Radical networking can prevent the often-isolated school leader from feeling as though she cannot have access to trusted individuals and resources. Radical networking happens when groups of individuals who share a common set of responsibilities build a formative and supportive network. Radical Principals construct these kinds of networks. They exist across space and time. Radical networks can occur in person, digitally, or in a hybrid format. They should not be costly. These are terrific alternatives to coaching or other expensive mentoring models. Building radical networks allows school leaders to employ strategies that motivate them to seek radical success. They include the hallmarks of self-care, and network care.

.

7

Radical Loyalty

A principal received a phone call with a shocking revelation about one of his teachers. A parent claimed that their son had been "struck across the face" by their middle school teacher. The teacher was a long-time veteran, respected among the school community, and the accusation was outrageous. Yet the parents were adamant. How could this be? The principal quickly arranged an investigation. What became clear has been a more common occurrence: the student had either lied about the accusation or misperceived the interaction so badly that he recalled it in a highly inaccurate manner. How could he be so off-base?

The parent was unbending; this had occurred. Under pressure, the principal could have given the vibe that he was keeping an open mind and notified the teacher with a non-supportive, "I'll have to look into this" tone That is not what radical loyalty nurtures. He knew it had not happened, and he knew he could get proof. All students in the class quickly confirmed the

DOI: 10.4324/9781003275718-7

teacher's attempt at a simple verbal redirection. Threatened by parents with a lawsuit, the principal stood by the truth and defended his teacher.

The principal believed firmly in the justice system, and in this teacher's innocence. The teacher never forgot how his principal handled this highly sensitive situation. Sure, our school leader received calls and emails contesting the return of this teacher to the classroom and contact from the press, even pressure from his superiors about urging him to play it conservatively. But that's not what Radical Principals do to bring about the kind of loyalty that pays back tenfold.

Radical Principals stand by their ethics, and fight for what is right. The moral course of action is often not the easiest route. But those who get caught in the crossfire remember if their leader stood by or stood up for them. Radical loyalty is born in moments like this. The teacher would climb Mount Everest for the principal if he asked. The accused had been through a trying ordeal and the incredible gratitude and support he experienced meant nothing would prevent him from doing the school leaders bidding.

One of the trademarks of a truly radical leader is having the ability to push people further than most are willing to go, past the comfort zone to change. This is the results of extreme loyalty they have earned. Radical loyalty does not happen overnight, or by accident, and most leadership books pile on theories about how a leader gains it. Yet there is a measured approach and an insight into seizing on the windows of opportunity that are the purest, most profound opportunities to achieve radical loyalty.

The characteristics of loyalty that allow a leader to confidently say to almost anyone in their organization, "if you trust me, then follow me," stands apart from textbook-defined loyalty. Radical loyalty is the kind you see when you do not quite understand why a leader is so magnetizing, so trusted and inspires such belief. She just has it. It happens in moments big and small. Being viewed as ethical is one factor. Fighting for ethics and the rights of others is what separates school leaders with the extreme trust they have gained from those who follow them.

This chapter explores why Radical Principals have the unique ability to gain extreme commitment from others, and how to get there. Illustrative storylines and evidence will assist in providing a practical understanding. This matters because a sense of ardent loyalty and how to employ it for optimal impact as leaders lays the groundwork for flourishing school communities.

Radical loyalty is crafted at a level Barnard refers to as the zone of indifference (Wood, 2013)—the degree of trust unconditionally given to leaders by their subordinates. When the zone of indifference is high, loyalty is directly proportional and school leaders are truly able to depend on their extraordinary allegiance to make radical changes. Getting there, not neglecting but protecting it, and applying it toward school and student success are imperative to achieving the degree of radical loyalty that results in students winning.

Radical loyalty almost never has anything to do with treating people with a flawless approach. In fact, assuming this and striving for it is both overwhelming and counterproductive. Consider measuring customer service satisfaction, to demonstrate the importance of responding to issues, rather than expecting unrealistic and unattainable perfection, as mentioned earlier about attaining organizational loyalty. You can achieve this through measuring with anonymous 360° school climate surveys (*Effective Principal 360°*, 2009).

The discoveries from this approach should influence every school leadership methodology. First, enchanting customers does not boost loyalty. Rather, decreasing the effort to get their problem resolved does. Lowering the resistance to resolution is what binds an individual to an organization, and their leader. Allowing bureaucratic systems to frustrate a quest toward solutions is a large part of what is discussed in this text. Working to strip these from processes, in subtle and obvious ways are important factors in getting radical loyalty well established.

Second, acting purposefully with this approach can greatly boost the perception of quality support, lower costs, and minimized customer agitation. Consider those costs, not just the capital funds. In education, we face resource and human costs. Reducing these costs increases success rates in ways that translate to possibilities for vibrant learning communities to flourish. Consider a principal, who faced a challenge, and how he worked to shift perspective, as the new building leader, and how his school gained the kind of momentum that builds from a foundation of radical loyalty.

If You Give a Mouse a Cookie…

The building principal was new, untested, and up against an old guard that had been hardened by an antagonistic relationship over nearly two decades with the previous administration. The union hardliners saw their role, as an "us-against-them" approach,. They wore this role as a badge of honor in the fight against their perspective of negative leadership. Clearly, our principal inherited a loyalty gap. For right or wrong, this was the position the faculty held in his newly adopted school, and it only served to hurt children who instead needed a cohesive school community to thrive in.

This "us-against-them" mentality aroused a distinctive, uneasy, and unfamiliar feeling for our new principal. This was unknown territory. He had been accustomed to being held in high regard, trusted and appreciated in his previous role as an assistant principal, teacher leader and staff developer, in his prior school community.

The encounter that ensued illustrates the challenge he was up against and how he was able to shift a tide that had been too obstructed, too untrusting, and too toxic for too long, fostering instead a nurturing learning environment for faculty and students in their school community.

A teacher came crying to the new principal, devastated by the mistreatment that she had been subject to at the hands of a colleague. While this other teacher was nontenured, she had an intimidating demeanor. Prior to the principal's arrival, she was expected to achieve tenure, in her final year of review. This presented a dilemma for the new principal as a teacher who would become a long-term challenge if granted tenure.

This third-year teacher had a reputation for being unkind and hurtful, something like an adult version of a mean-girl. This teacher had thrown her colleague under the bus, for something she was not responsible for. Regardless of what the matter was about, our mean girl approached this situation deviously, was nasty and of greatest concern, had the pizazz to pull it off. Learning about this injustice at the hands of a kind, sensitive, caring and less assertive teacher compelled the new principal to act.

It was at this inopportune time that the faculty union stepped in, defiantly defending their mean girl. They were far less concerned, or oblivious to her behavior, and the harmful impact she had on others than they were about defending her. This mentality dangerously reinforced mediocrity and impacted school climate in ways that pushed most well-intentioned professionals further away.

At the very least, it inhibited their ability to replace these destructive behaviors with productive ones, which could have helped to build a better school community for all. The majority of decent, well intentioned faculty felt isolated because teachers like the mean girl had been granted impunity. Indeed, the loud, assertively combative teachers wielded the sword of influence, one that reinforced mediocrity Radical Principals must consciously and cleverly fight against this every day.

Our new principal showed respect for the intended purpose of having association representation. He recognized and valued many strong teachers were deeply involved in the union leadership and strived to build bonds of trust with them. He recalled a mentor once advising him about how to approach union leadership. Do whatever you can to work with and resolve issues with your association, support them when they are right, but stand up and fight the right battles for children and adults when they are wrong. Do not shy away. Do not let them confuse kindness for weakness.

Calling her conduct into question, the principal arranged to officiate a meeting with this teacher, and her association representative. It became evident that the representative was focused on intimidation tactics toward him and attempted to call the shots. He was pressured to adjust what he had memorialized in a letter of reprimand issued to the mean girl, an effect that had he agreed to, would have removed the weight behind his correspondence. This would have shielded the mean girl, causing no real resolution or accountability to hold her responsible or enact change.

After the meeting came to an end and he refused to be influenced to change the language of the letter, he was uncertain of what might happen next. It was the kind of risk a nontenured, new and unproven principal was certain to lose sleep over. He only knew that it was the right thing to do, so he remained committed to the decision.

He recalled advice from another mentor: put your beliefs out in front of your faculty, every day. Would he somehow be penalized or reduced to nonaction by faculty pushing back in an organized protest, or by his own superintendent questioning his judgment? It was an unsettling feeling, but he stuck to his principles.

A faculty meeting was on the horizon, just days away. As word spread of the disciplinary meeting, and how he had stood up to the union, details of what had happened emerged. Unfortunately, most of these were inaccurate details. There was no mention about his defense of the innocent teacher-victim and our intimidated teacher also kept her mouth shut for fear of repercussions.

At faculty meetings, the principal had employed motivational activities to engage his faculty. This included offering lottery trivia to winners who might have their duty period covered or the chance to win a premier parking spot. Engagement mattered. His intention was to make faculty meetings feel less like meetings of compliance, where faculty are lectured to, and more like interactive, participatory, and fun opportunities that helped inspire teachers to work together as a collective to develop creative ideas about teaching and learning.

Understandably confused, many of the faculty who had developed a positive relationship with their new principal were instructed to act in defiance: *when the principal hands you a cookies at the faculty meeting, refuse to take one, as a symbol of protest.* The principal received word moments before the meeting that this was about to happen, unbelievably childish as it sounded. His big tray of cookies would go noticeably untouched. He had to think quickly on his feet. How would this unfold? What would people think? It is moments like these, big and small, that define a school culture, and, just as importantly, how a leader responds to meet the moment.

Thinking fast, the principal opened a couple of large cookie containers and pulled out a handful from each of them. This way, he contemplated, if no one took any, at least it would look as though some had been taken. A bit sneaky? Yes. Strategic? Definitely! As the faculty steadily streamed in to the large group meeting room, the old guard drifted past, appearing to slow down to a full stop at the cookie container, only to drift on. Then a few newer faculty members, apparently naïve to the politics (or uninterested) unfolding, and with a big midafternoon appetite, grabbed a couple, claiming "oh cool, chewy, warm cookies!"

The meeting proceeded as the principal could feel the chill in the room. Yet he did not mention one word about the cookies, or politics or protests. He proceeded with his meeting and the faculty sat, mostly indifferent, if not silent. It was a somber mood, but he maintained his professional demeanor. The next day, a wise, and influential, member of his faculty privately reached out. She said,

> Jaimie, I am not sure what happened yesterday at the faculty meeting, but we were told under no circumstances to take a cookie, some sort of a protest. I really didn't know what it was about, and I felt pressured to go along. I shouldn't have. I didn't have the whole story and I don't think you are a bad person. I am ashamed of my behavior. Please accept my apology, I think you have done an excellent job bringing our building together, in a short time.

An opportunity was born. Many angry, reactive bosses might instinctively snap back with, "You should have known better!" (and a surprising number do), or would ignore the message all together, going silent. This leader did something that sparked a radical moment. His response:

> Thank you for the note. It meant so much to me. I wanted you to know that the cookies are still fresh, so I put one in your box this morning. There is nothing attached to it. I just thought you might still enjoy it.

Consider his response. He did not ask her to go back to her colleagues and advertise what a nice guy he was, or that they got it all wrong (although he wanted to). He did not make a statement to the whole faculty that "Some of you just don't know what the good people think and feel." That was it. Nothing more. What he did not know or expect was what would happen next.

This teacher told everyone. What a real, down-to-earth guy our boss is! There was no ulterior motive. No pressure, no hidden agenda. Just an olive branch. That peace offering would reach long and wide, and for years to come. This principal learned a valuable lesson about the experience: how small, strategically timed moves can have such a massive impact. These impacts can produce huge payoffs, if handled carefully.

It is only human nature in situations like this that our pride invokes primal, unproductive reactions. Yet it is best to set our pride aside, and to deliver responses that result in incredibly fair more consequential outcomes. This takes practice and happens in difficult, unpredictable moments. The reward is too great, and the change that takes place too invaluable to consider falling prey to our most primitive instincts of defensiveness.

Balancing Loyalty and the Leader's Ego

A famous writer, well known for his collection of short stories from *The Jungle Book* (1894), which was also featured as a movie wrote a poem quite titled "If" in 1910. This poem characterizes one's ideal aspirations to become a better version of oneself, as readers are guided on a path for how to deal with different complications in life. Rudyard Kipling (Poets.org—Academy of American Poets, n.d.) wrote on how to triumph, and how to be a supremely decent human being. This poem can be searched online and is cited in the bibliography.

The first section of the poem has great implications for Radical Principals, since leaders have their ego tested regularly, sometimes beyond their capacity to be able to refrain from a reflexive reaction. One principal posted the first stanza of the poem on her office wall. This section is a testament to her leadership, the maintenance of her humility, and managing her self-regulation through the struggles all leaders are inevitably confronted with.

The opening line characterizes the importance of keeping a level head, even as others around you are unable to do so. While other people are quick to blame you (the leader), do not fall victim to this same reaction. Forge ahead with belief in yourself, even as other people express pessimism and doubt you.

Humility involves a provision of acceptance for others doubting. This mirrors Grant's (2021) emphasis on the value of humility, which challenges a person to be more self-aware. Humility can be accomplished by identifying what you don't know and recognizing your blind spots before they serve as a catalyst in causing you complications beyond your control.

Kipling proceeds with advice to practice patience and to prevent oneself from becoming fatigued by a tolerance toward others' limiting behaviors, and hence their struggles with invoking radical change. The radical leader is challenged to remain objective while others are lying about them, and to avoid matching those lies. He highlights the necessity of maturity by choosing not to be hateful of others. As a leader, modeling this compassion with the humblest of emphasis means not being trapped by conceit; by not acting as though you look better than others or talking in condescending ways to them.

Radical loyalty is earned by leaders who show their vulnerable humanity, especially by espousing their own great humility. A modest approach makes leaders appear humane to others, and those within organizations place high value on this kind of a leader. This is evidenced in an abundance of research. Yet even the humblest among radical leaders have their humility tested.

In a world pressured by instant, "always-on" answers and results, the tension can squeeze a leader to react, rather than using a proactive mindset. When pressure clouds mindset, we are challenged to lose focus. Staying conscientious of this vulnerability helps leaders to maintain perspective.

The reason it is so difficult to sustain ego is because we tend to be physiologically hardwired to believe that the world revolves around each of us. This relates to the fight or flight instinct within this hardwiring, something far less practical in present day than when human 'struggled for survival.

This is counterproductive in contemporary leadership because selfishness holds us back from long-term success. Our primal defenses are inclined to blow everything out of proportion, be it good or bad, and to be biased toward ourselves. It is these extremes that get us away from a level of cognition that engages our radical thought processes. We are left thinking too much with our primal brain region (the back), versus the higher critical thinking region (the front).

The problem with this is the emotional roller coaster ride we get caught up on. If things are going well, we might mistakenly attribute some degree of luck to success. High on success, our vision becomes too clouded. We prematurely assume that we must be doing something right and that we are more responsibility for that success then we may be when going well.

When this exaggerated narrative starts to take hold, we are unprepared for the inevitable challenges on the downside every leader faces in the ebbs and flows, the ups and downs that we naturally cycle through. This inhibits our ability to learn and develop from regular challenges. When striving to be a radical leader, being aware of these hurdles allows us to offset the disadvantages originating in our primal instincts. That is why ego is such a big challenge for all individuals to overcome, including, and I would argue especially leaders, with more given power.

More on Ego

No great leader stands on solid footing 100% of the time. Expecting a smooth ride is impractical. Every exceptional leader is prone to difficult moments, especially when they are under tremendous amounts of pressure or when the leader faces a distinct injustice. Recognizing and accepting limitations helps leaders to become better at preparing for the trials, and, at least as important, being able to move on from them.

Exceptional leaders understand that the first step in managing their ego is to acknowledge their deficiencies. They are able to avoid hypocritically pretentious behavior, such as ignoring the reality that this part of their psyche does not exist or can be easily dealt with. They respect and are honest about their imperfections, even if it means having to face harsh realities when they look in the mirror.

Using Ego to Earn Radical Loyalty

Being an educational leader qualifies Radical Principals to model the greatest gift education can offer: how to become lifelong learners. Establishing this allows school leaders to use their ego for the better. They accept that they are always learning, constantly given the opportunity to Think Again (Grant, 2021). We can demonstrate for others why this approach propels us to achieve remarkable heights and for others to come along for the ride.

One of the most destructive impacts to loyalty is when ego causes leaders to turn off feedback. This results in reduced organizational input, to such a negligible or nonexistent amount that the values around the school become hierarchical, instead of transformational. Feedback serves functional purposes for longevity and each of these connect to loyalty.

First, allowing a free flow of feedback makes individuals feel as if they are heard, even if their idea is not endorsed, or not totally adopted. By having a voice, they are empowered, and willing to support the leader. If their principal were to go into a harmful direction, those offering feedback are likely to step in to help their leader put on the brakes. Consider the quote, "leaders who don't listen will eventually be surrounded by people who don't speak" (Andy Stanley). There is probably no greater challenge to achieving vigorous loyalty than feeling silenced.

Second, allowing a free flow of feedback boosts the likelihood that new and groundbreaking ideas are born, by way of the *multiplier effect*. Consider the premise: leaders who advocate for groupthink allow trials by people to be explored and even applied in practice. Multipliers get more accomplished by leveraging the intelligence and capabilities of the people around them. This logic may sound obvious but consider the opposite kind of leader and his impact, the *diminisher*. This kind of leader surprisingly persists among many organizations, and their influence is toxic.

Diminisher leaders believe their intellect is exceptional, giving them the illusion that they are the only one capable of creating good ideas and successfully running the organization. A focus on their own perceived genius and their determination to appear as the smartest person in the room has a diminishing effect on everyone around them. For them to look intelligent, others must be seen as deficient in comparison. This attitude inhibits them from permitting others to have a voice. It reduces their willingness for what they can offer to the organization.

Most among us have experienced working with multiplier and diminisher leaders. It is easy to distinguish the levels of loyalty granted to each. Multipliers are out there, but it seems as though too many diminishers endure in leadership. In addition to the loyalty curve and how positively this impacts multiplier leaders, consider a study which demonstrated that multipliers garnered 100% more output from their employees than their diminisher counterparts (Foster & Wiseman, 2014). As leaders, it is our job to balance our own skill set with the talents of others, especially when a better idea can generate from others, and produces double the output!

Not Everyone Will Come on Board, and That's Okay

Leaders who aim to be pleasers struggle with the reality that while 90% of their faculty may trust and feel loyalty toward them, they worry about the other 10%. No matter what, this minority will find a way to challenge them, put them down, or make them feel like an inferior leader. This group may possess influence in your school, sometimes even greater than their leader. They should be classified as a loser support group—dangerous but few and keeping them in that category creates a more benign effect in dealing with their negative and toxic impact.

While this is a group that must be managed by the radical leader, they should not be a focus group to achieve radical loyalty from. They are also part of a leader's ego self-management. Every successful leader can immediately refer to that group who were good at being awful and at making others feel diminished themselves.

This group should be dealt with very differently from the masses. They must not be part of a leader's quest to achieve radical loyalty, because the efficiency factor is too low. It is beyond the point of diminishing return. The leader must not allow this group to influence their wellbeing in a way that causes harm to the whole. These priorities are non-negotiable.

Most of those representing this group are not truly bad people. They are simply part of that loser support group which validates their feelings of ineffectiveness. While the leader needs to be careful not to highlight their deficiencies in negative ways, she should recognize that many in this group simply suffer from factors that impair their judgment, such as one referred to as the *shadow effect*.

Difficult people are all around us and most negatively influence due to their shadow effect on us. A person's shadow side is primitive, negative energy and is impulsive. Factors like rage, envy, greed, and selfishness are components of the shadow side. We all have a shadow side. The difference is to what degree this shadow side is consciously projected onto others. These are the parts we disassociate from ourselves, that we no longer accept to be of our own making. We find ways to blame others and other factors, rather than associating these with internal factors, those that ironically give us more control to address these shadow effects.

Negative group members are highly reinforced by implementing a shadow effect. They become masters at blame displacement and handing off responsibility. We see these individuals everywhere. In our own families, perhaps among struggling friends, and at our places of work. When they impair a leader's ability to make radical change for the benefit of children, we must be masters of our own energy to address them, while not falling into the trap of matching their shadow behavior.

A shadow self is part of human nature because we are all prone to primal defenses that were designed to keep us evolutionarily safe long before running water, shelter, accessible food supplies and education reduced the need for humans to live in survival mode, from one hunted meal to the next.

Individuals who are emotionally intelligent, and more keenly self-aware can combat and put these primitive thoughts aside, pragmatically shrugging them off for the more functional modern version of mindfulness. Unless we do deliberative work on our shadow selves, this shadow projects onto others. If that happens, we persistently assign someone or something else the blame, so we do not have to own it.

Identifying individuals with significant shadow effect behaviors enables leaders to minimize their impact, while as importantly gaining and sustaining radical loyalty and trust from the majority. While many difficult individuals are often the loudest voices, we can more effectively quiet them, or help others shut off their noise, when we model how to balance our ego with effects from these individuals. It is easy to be trapped by them because they attempt to seize onto our pride, capturing our attention in strongly instinctive ways.

You know the personality of individuals with an overbearing shadow side. They seek attention through guilt, and if you are not careful, you will be doing their work for them, or, worse, cleaning it up. You may even have it flipped onto you as if it is somehow your responsibility, rather than theirs. If you are not cautious, they will shift the monkey from their back onto yours (Whitaker et al., 2020). Before you know it, you are validating this with excuses like, "it's easier for me to do it for them…"

While you will find little success achieving any degree of loyalty, let alone radical loyalty from this group, you need to recognize their power plays. That is why achieving radical loyalty comes with an acute awareness of these individuals, how they hold sway, how not to get sucked into their influence, and how best to redirect energy from them, toward the majority, who are ready and willing to be loyal. They are the ones who deserve your time and dedication. The rest deserve a trained eye on managing any attempt they employ to redirect responsibility and blame.

A large part of the productivity resulting from radical loyalty includes constructing limitations around those accustomed to successfully infringing on others' space and time. This is because the group majority who are not trying to take advantage appreciate your testament to accountability.

In fact, it is often why shadow-side individuals attempt to manipulate everyone around them, by making you feel ineffective, and not worthy of their loyalty. Somehow, you are to blame for their ills. If you can keep perspective and model a balance that enables you to hold them accountable in an objective way, just as you would anyone else, your faculty will take notice and value your professional savvy and redirection for how you reduced the influence of these shadow individuals. That breeds a quieting influence among your followers that results in radical loyalty.

Summary

Radical loyalty is not easily earned, and it happens in windows of opportunity that must be seized on. These are often missed by "good enough" leaders and that is a terrible error. Taking advantage of moments to earn radical loyalty from their following allows school leaders to gain support and trust by their faculty and school community that enables them to move toward radical achievement in their school.

The characteristics of loyalty that allow a leader to risk saying to almost anyone in their organization, "if you trust me, then follow me," stands apart from textbook defined loyalty. A mentality that reinforces mediocrity is what impacts school climate in ways that push most well-intentioned professionals away.

At the very least, it inhibits their ability to replace these destructive distractions and help to build a better school community.

Moments, both big and small, define a school culture, and, as importantly, how a leader responds to them. Small, strategic moves can have a massive impact, when you least expect it, so keep chiseling away. Humility is so critical to radical success for school leaders that practicing it and being aware of our limitations is prudent. Recognizing and accepting limitations helps leaders to become better at preparing for the trials, and at least as important, being able to move on from them.

Leaders accepting feedback results in two major benefits: First, feedback helps act as a dragnet, catching potential mistakes a leader may make, and those who trust they can alert their leader will help prevent such a mistake. Second, allowing others the invitation to share ideas without fear of reprisal fosters a multiplier effect, increasing the likelihood radical ideas are born. Multiplier leaders represent a contradiction to many leaders known as diminishers, who silence others to pacify their ego.

Be mindful and aware of the loser support group in your school, keep them small and insignificant by seizing their power through the radical loyalty offered by most.

8

Institutionalizing Equity

Applying Practices to Reverse Cycles of Injustice

Having established numerous radical formulas for school communities, we call upon further action steps needed to generate the probability for sustained and sensational change. Radical Principals seize on the moment, stepping into opportunities, bringing a trusting community along with them. This is an extraordinary new era for the school community, which can now shine as a beacon, as an inspirational model for others.

To institutionalize something is not a bad idea ... it is *what* we institutionalize that matters. In radically-led schools, you hear the stories where, against all odds, history is reversed, and impoverished or troubled organizations, overwhelmed with challenges, begin to show remarkable progress. This does not happen by accident or luck, nor overnight. This happens when school leaders take on the kinds of schemes contained in this text, based on research and experience, to methodically produce results that would have otherwise seemed improbable. They institutionalize equity, for all.

DOI: 10.4324/9781003275718-8

Consider one school which was confronted with the brutal fact that its staff were suspending twice as many children of color as they were white children. Unfortunately, this is an all too consistent pattern. A closer look at why this is so devastating should be examined before considering the unique ways to alter this trajectory permanently.

Black high school students are suspended at twice the rate (12.8%) as their white (6.1%) or Hispanic (6.3%) peers nationally (Kamenetz, 2018). Aside from an alarmingly disproportionate rate, the reality is just how detrimental suspension is, for all students. Not just for those that are suspended, but for everyone; the entire school community, including those not disciplined, are negatively affected by students being disproportionately and exceedingly suspended.

Research reinforces that suspending students has minimal or even negative impact on changing behavior for disciplined students. Incredibly, the consequences of suspension reach far beyond the effects of one student. A punitive climate affects everyone in the school community. Additionally, academic achievement gains are poorer among suspended and non-suspended peers. That's right, non-suspended individuals are also negatively impacted. Perceptions of school climate are negative. Additionally, longer discipline cycles result in increasingly more harmful consequences on a student's future academic performance, attendance, and behavior (Álvarez, 2021).

The evidence is overwhelming and an exasperating cycle revealed through longitudinal evidence reinforces the same challenges. This may make well-intended professionals wonder, if we have known for decades that suspension does not work, and if it is even more profound for students of color, we must examine why we continue doing it. While suspensions have trended downward in recent years, the declines are not significant enough and the inequity divide remains at double the rate between students of color and their white peers (Zill & Wilcox, 2019).

Various reasons suggest why we persist with the same punitive approach even though it is quite plainly not working. Doing the same thing and expecting different results is the true definition of insanity. One of the strongest reasons for the stubborn insistence to suspend as a consequence is due to deeply institutionalized practices. Schools often face very little leverage in implementing new, potentially controversial, or untested practices, and non-punitive alternatives are often met with resistance by many in the school community.

These barriers persist; and they have served as one of the main reasons for the inspiration of this book. We can, in fact, alter this trajectory once and for all. Administrators will likely provide a host of ideas they wanted to try a different approach but were quickly met with bureaucratic resistance and institutional blockades. The other reason? It is what we have always done and remains an accepted practice, by traditionalists in the community, board of education members, even lawyers and judges ruling on disciplinary outcomes, throughout the course of history within school case law contexts.

The Solution

Previously, the mantra to beg for forgiveness rather than ask for permission was presented. Radical schools and their leaders take these kinds of risks, led by the audacity of their Radical Principal. Doing so is the only option for reversing the course on school discipline, and specifically to contest the status quo of unequal discipline on disadvantaged populations.

While alternative interventions to suspension are transferable strategies, the important ideology is that the additive effect of having a collection of these options available is the true difference maker. One of the themes in this text has been that bundling, compounding, or stacking interventions or ideas is what builds momentum, rather than banking on any one silver bullet.

Indeed, a series of compounding, composite ideas available at the Radical Principals' disposal are the agents of true and sustainable change. Counting on a solo idea would not be nearly as detrimental as suspending students, but also not nearly as effective as the compound effect of intertwining interventions, weaving them together to impact change more tightly. Have this stack of composite ideas available as options to select from and weave them in and out in the right circumstances. Following are some innovative methods and programs to consider in implementing this approach.

Perception Is More Powerful That Fact

How does a school leader get her faculty to see past their own justifications for students who misbehave facing penalties rather than learning interventions? The expectation they look back at and get stuck on the problem, instead of forward toward the future is in itself a problem. In one school, many of the faculty still had deeply embedded subconscious biases that were systemically reinforced. How did the school leader get them to recognize the damaging effects their personal biases brought on, resulting in often-unintended participation in discriminatory practices? When can the tide shift, toward a better, fairer, more equitable school community for all?

Provided next are examples of ways in which Radical Principals lead with bravery and determination, balanced with patience and timing, to deploy extraordinary techniques which, stacked together, change their school communities. The best part? When school leaders institutionalize equity, everyone wins. All children. All school community members. A better school community for all has an impact that is harmonious, replicable, and compounded. It is a celebration of achievement that permeates deeply in the lives of those who are part of the community.

There are three primary practices for radical leaders to forge this path of success and equity with for all:

1. Professional Development
2. Leading by example (implementing programs)
3. Teaching students' self-regulation strategies to propel them beyond disadvantage

Professional Development

One of the most impactful ways to support the professional growth of educators is through meaningful, empowering, and invigorating professional learning experiences. This can be accomplished by arranging eventful thought-out professional development, like Edcamps, such as "un-faculty meetings" (Gaskell, 2020).

Traditional faculty meetings are often held at the worst time of the day, and this has been revealed in research (Byrne, 2017). While adjusting the time to offer professional development is difficult, confronting the challenge by fostering motivational, revitalizing experiences is the answer in reversing the effects of low-energy cycles of unproductive meetings.

By generating practices that present high interest choices for teachers, we can switch off low-motivation states and gain from the opportunity, rather than go up against the grumbling arguments about a long day and a wasted hour. Arranging faculty meetings so teachers are more vibrant, directly involved, interested and relevant, like Edcamps, are the building blocks for this framework. See Appendix C for more information on creating your own Edcamp-style, faculty meeting.

Structure lively, conference style drop-in/out meetings that faculty look forward to. Offer a menu of opportunities and connect these to relevant professional goals.: These should also be framed around student achievement and success. Gain consensus that improving instruction, classroom management, student performance and family relations are the moniker under which we serve virtually all else for teaching and learning. Teachers can gain valued professional development from this set of values and structures.

Solicit teachers to enlist best practices around a theme that shape the conference-style format. This adds to the flow and energy of the experience. Teachers appreciate and value that their colleagues can offer relevant resources and ideas, from within the trenches more than theory or ivory tower declarations.

Enlisting and rewarding faculty for sharing their ideas also eliminates the problem of a great idea being lost, buried in a corner of the school that never got promoted for the greater good as solid practice, that can reach more classrooms, teachers and most of all, students. Idea sharing, and gaining from concepts like the multiplier effect comes from these refreshing opportunities, getting idea sharing off the ground and beyond limited spaces.

Connect Science and Story Together to Get Faculty on Board

Another aspect of professional development that has proven to play a pivotal role in moving faculty to support disadvantaged students is by sharing not just science, or story, but both, interconnected together to package a convincing rationale for helping children overcome the odds they face. Discussing these at opportune times of the year and in moments when faculty can best use the information makes timing an integral part of this delivery process.

Integrating story into processes of professional development and during classroom lessons is an effective strategy for retention of content. The human brain is engineered to interpret and retrieve content from stories far more efficiently than exclusively fact-based information. How does this happen?

How Storylines Make a Stronger Neural Connection

When you hear a story, your brainwaves quite literally mirror those of the storyteller. Interpreting narrative triggers areas of the mind involved in decoding and visualizing a person's motives and perspective. Story is so much more economical in delivering a message because of this matching effect between the storyteller and receiver.

Capitalizing on this, consider the message conveyed to educators returning to classrooms with disadvantaged children. Provided are a sampling of compelling storylines to capitalize on with the powerful effect that matching brain waves between teller and receiver has.

Connecting through Storylines

Three Letters from Teddy Roy (Ballard, 2002). Warning: this tearjerker is based on a true and remarkable story; a testament to the incredible impact for how we connect. The story opens with a description of Teddy, a child who began his elementary years with some promise. Then, like many others, he faced a traumatic experience that caused him to decline, without the resources to recover.

The sudden and painful loss of his mother changed a pleasant, energetic child, into a disaffected, failing, disheveled, and less likable student. His father was emotionally detached, and Teddy often fell asleep in class, inattentive, unprepared, and out of touch. Teddy's teacher recalls striking red Xs all over his paper and doing so with an almost sadistic pleasure. Upon review of his files, his fifth-grade teacher discovered the sudden and unexpected loss of his mother as a cause for his downward spiral. Meanwhile, as the winter holidays approached, she held her annual holiday event with her class.

A gift exchange commenced as the teacher gave prizes to students and she opened gifts their parents had selected for her, until it was time to open Teddy's. The gift was wrapped in a brown paper bag. Several students snickered as she unwrapped it and revealed the contents. Inside was a partially filled bottle of perfume and a broken bracelet. The teacher put them both on, remarking how she loved the gifts he gave her, putting on her best poker face. As the classroom emptied for the holiday, Teddy stayed back and before departing said, "You smell just like my mother."

Moments like these are what defines purpose for so many teachers and is often why they say they are so richly rewarded, if not financially so. It is not by money but by having the chance to help a child, to see their potential in far richer ways that teachers have the power to be rewarded and help.

She bawled for nearly an hour after Teddy's departure, went home, and determined to seize on this as an opportunity to help him turn everything around, any way she could when they returned in the New Year. From January through June, the teacher stayed after school daily with Teddy, supporting and giving him love and attention beyond the school day.

The story continues as Teddy moves on through the years, as the teacher receives letters of progress from him telling her about his high school graduation, and how he eventually became a doctor. Over the years, his final letter was a special request. He was getting married! He asked if his former teacher would sit at his wedding in the place that would have been his mother's?

Certainly, this account speaks volumes about the power of a teacher having a change of heart. As important is the context for sharing a story like this. If we can help reframe teacher's perspectives about difficult and challenging students, we can reclaim a starting place to help so many disadvantaged children. See reference (Ballard, 2002) in the bibliography for access to the full-length original story.

The Pygmalion Effect. This message is based on a research study and the connection for faculty should be powerful. Consider the context: In the 1960s, a team of researchers (Rosenthal and Jacobsen, 1968) selected students, who were reported to be gifted.

Teachers were notified at the beginning of the year of this "high performing group."

On the other hand, other students were among those identified to be average performers. Teachers were likewise notified of this group of so-so academic performers. In truth, all students were average performers, including the group claimed to be high achievers, but the teachers did not know this.

What was remarkable was that the group that were perceived as high performers significantly outperformed their peers, even though they should not have excelled and achieved at the extraordinarily higher level they did. They were performing at heights that mirrored gifted students, despite their records indicating they were average like the rest.

Several factors contributed to what pushed the perceived high-performing group to greater levels of success. These included teachers unknowingly providing this group with:

◆ more personal attention,
◆ deeper feedback,
◆ more support, and
◆ positive affirmations.

On the other hand, teachers generally attended to the perceived lower performing students at lower rates, offering them less personal attention, and they performed predictably lower

While this study was conducted over a half century ago, Portell (2021, 29:49) discusses how the Pygmalion effect is alive and well today, due to perceptions among teachers and the influence of their own backgrounds, causing them to be effected by experiential bias. This phenomenon results in a processing limitation, caused by our brain, which is designed to access information in an efficient set of patterns. Indeed, prior evidence cited provides a convincing argument, about why disproportionate discipline rates for students of color are the result among numerous other factors.

This reveals that the Pygmalion effect has persisted far beyond a study conducted over a half century ago, and therefore has incredible relevance as to how we convey awareness of these factors today. Indeed, inequity exists and illuminating these to counteract them for adults in ways they cannot see is urgently necessary. Sharing the story of the Pygmalion effect is one of these counteractors.

These interventions must be part of every school's radical professional development program. Sharing storylines like these should happen at the start of a school year, during mid-year slumps, and in continuous cycles to break the systemic barriers fortifying perceptual inequities.

The Children of Kauai

A longitudinal study over four decades followed the lives of hundreds of individuals, from birth through mid-life. An extraordinary outcome resulted for a large percentage of these children, who all had the indicators to fail (Werner & Smith, 2001). Indeed, they were at risk, and disadvantaged, set up for a predictable pattern of failure. A team of scientists embarked on this massive and extraordinary longitudinal study of individuals, from childbirth through middle age. It highlighted the power of resilience, upon a remarkable accidental byproduct of the study, discovered unexpectedly.

The reason this study is so invaluable to share with educators is because it illustrates how a large subgroup demonstrated remarkable success, despite the odds that they should never have. Among 200 children who were identified as at risk, one-third demonstrated exceptional resilience through post-traumatic growth responses, as opposed to post traumatic stress responses. How? Three clusters of factors were identified, which remain incredibly relevant and applicable today.

1. *Protective factors within the individual.* These individuals had fostered a persistence to the challenges that they were surrounded by. They serve as a model for students learning to self-regulate, a skill highlighted here for students to look past their own disadvantages and to aim for opportunities beyond their current limitations.
2. *Protective factors of surrogate support.* Substitute caregivers, mentors, coaches, and teachers were those that served as replacement parent figures, adult mentors in the lives of these disadvantaged children. This posits a strong justification for why mentoring is so effective, necessary, and invaluable to implement in schools today.
3. *Protective factors in the community.* Affiliation was a critical component in students connecting with their community. Being on a team, connected to a religious affiliation, a school club, or any organized group provided these children with a sense of belonging.

Adding more inspiration to this storyline: these individuals were able to seize on a variety of moments, or windows of opportunity, propelling them beyond their at-risk status. In other words, there was no specific timetable they had to escape from their path to forge a sustained, successful, life-long experience. They could turn it around as late as young adulthood to experience their own post-traumatic growth. Conveying this as an "it's-never-too-late" theme has incredible implications for recognizing we can help students at any age, not by predestined time limits.

More on Storytelling, From Within

Educators are primed by their nature and training to be excellent storytellers. They often narrate as they integrate stories seamlessly into their classroom practice for learners. How often do teachers recall using stories to bridge a concept or break away for an important moment as they recount while they literally watch kids' eyes glaze over as they fade into their story?

They are captured by the rich and powerful contexts portrayed. Story has such a profound impact that an effectively delivered one can reframe an individual's personal view: shifting stubborn cognitive biases that persists in the wake of inequity. If we can influence adults and students in school with the power of story, this can be used to help them see past their biases and realize the potential within all children.

Example: One Educator's Story

Virtually every educator has a history that involves working through a tremendous challenge, achieving beyond expectation, or overcoming a major obstacle. These should be shared when possible, especially when an adult made it through their own vulnerabilities. One Radical Principal engages his faculty to illustrate this point. A respected, long-time leader, the mystery was revealed in the challenges that he had overcome, one day.

Well dressed, with an advanced degree hanging from his office wall, it was illogical to look at the success of this well-respected leader and consider the possibility that he was the same student who had failed high school math, twice. His challenges began far earlier. In elementary school, he was evaluated by the school psychologist. The report was deplorable, to say the least. He had been characterized as a student exhibiting developmental delays, hostility, impulsiveness, lacking in social awareness, and performing at far below grade level.

Being counted out early in life, he was characterized by this poor prognosis and the prospects looked dim. He was expected to fail. Yet he didn't. How? This is a story of a leader who unexpectedly rose above his limitations. Identifying why and how he managed to excel against the odds is an inspirational story and allows many children and the adults who teach them to see that even a highly successful grown-up can come from an unlikely childhood plagued by challenges. We all love an underdog story, because it gives us hope, and that hope can be translated to children in need.

Sharing this with others who would not expect this level of struggle from a successful school leader is not only courageous; it also helps show adults that disadvantaged students can aspire to new heights too. It models the way for teachers to share their own vulnerabilities and limitations and that, despite these, they are able to overcome and persevere as well. What a wonderful and relatable way to teach children who need it most. Allowing students to see the most vulnerable side of ourselves does not make us weak or exposed. Rather children, especially those who struggle have newfound respect for their positive role models, and the possibilities for them to overcome too.

Many individuals can attest to the remarkable success they rose to, despite obstacles that doomed them to likely failure. The odds against them, they can relate how they overcome these significant disadvantages. These persons captivate us by their perseverance, and resilience, as they overcome the odds.

While post-traumatic stress causes the damaging effects of traumatic experiences, post-traumatic growth serves as a healthier, more productive way forward from the struggles endured by trauma. This leader who struggled shares his story with faculty, in the context of never giving up on any challenged or difficult child, under any circumstance.

His obstacles were far greater than one could imagine, especially those who had come to know and trust him as an adult and their respected leader. Our most challenged students, and those under the most difficult circumstances, share a similar set of experiences, and connecting them to storylines shows possibilities rather than limitations.

Playing Your Hand

A principal recalls a great teacher he worked with several years ago, one who exemplified strength and inspiration. She had a legendary way of bringing out the best in kids, told in many accounts over the years. A "tough as nails" delivery was the kind of tough love that held her students to a higher standard than they themselves knew they were capable of. She worked with disadvantaged children. One of her favorite responses to students who wanted to give up, or to blame their failure on someone or something else was to "play the cards you are dealt."

Her point: we are all dealt a hand in life for which we have no control over. Some are fortunate to be dealt the hand that favors them with unadulterated benefits. Others fall somewhere in the middle. The rest, the children in most need, face seemingly insurmountable circumstances.

She was able to show these students that they had a choice: they can sit and suffer, complaining about their plight, or they can work from where they are, to seize any opportunity, small or large, that comes their way, to gain big dividends in the process. We are all dealt a hand. It is not the hand we are dealt, but rather how we play it that makes the difference in which course we take from that point of origin and, more importantly, where it leads us.

No matter how small, how insignificant, children do encounter these choices along the way. Certainly, the options they are offered are not the same as more privileged individuals. Yet they still have possibilities. How will they respond? This is an important outlook to convey and helping children see this way to gain for their own empowerment and success is significant.

Earlier chapters in this text focused on ways Radical Principals can restructure the impasses that inhibit opportunity for growth among children who face institutionalized limitations in their opportunities. This section examines how students can help themselves overcome the hindrances around them. These are both those circumstances that may appear beyond their control, and those that are self-induced.

What a liberating realization it is to discover that one can take back control of their conditions to propel beyond what stifles progress. Let us examine some ways we can help students learn how to self-regulate so that they can excel, not despite themselves, but because of how they mastered how to become the best version of themselves.

Teachers should view their role for how they support children as facilitators, and this is significant when helping them see what power they hold in their life. One of the most impactful ways to do this, given the more fragile circumstances many disadvantaged children are working around, is through thoughtful feedback.

Often, well-intended educators miss the mark on this opportunity because of how they deliver feedback, rather than what they say specifically. Properly orchestrated, feedback can serve as a catalyst for students to navigate around their hurdles, in monumental ways that far exceed what may seem like nothing more than informal feedback.

Consider a study, in which participants received feedback in two very different ways. In the first: one group was given positive feedback by a superior who displayed contrarily flat affect, and negative nonverbal body language. The second group were given feedback on their performance that was critical; even negative. However, this group was issued the response in a pleasant, more transparent way and with a positive, supportive tone. Group two reported a far more beneficial reception toward their meetings than the first group. They even expressed positive well-being resulting from this feedback.

Teachers can deliver feedback that is encouraging, nurturing and supportive, while developmentally and constructively motivating. This aids in the progress of students, as recipients of transparent feedback which is well issued, yet candid about how they can improve their performance. This feedback is even more profound for disadvantaged students, who are accustomed to unwelcome news without offering support or resources and need a supportive adult to manage and deliver it more readily.

In addition to delivering feedback which stimulates student responsiveness, educators should consider approaches that provoke self-reflection and control: Coyle (2013) refers to a study in which one phrase, just 19 words, increased student growth by an astonishing 40%, among white students. The phrase is simply: *I'm giving you these comments because I have very high expectations and I know that you can reach them.*

More remarkable? Students of color responded to the same feedback at a rate of 320% growth. While the 40% increase is impressive, 320% is astonishing. It is possible to infer that the even larger increase among students of color was the result of these students receiving the feedback in such a way that they do not normally have access to, and that this in turn releases them from inhibitions toward accelerated growth and development.

Recall that students of color are disciplined at a disproportionately higher rate than their white peers. Reversing this trend suggests that these students have an exponentially greater response to the kind of supportive feedback they may not regularly receive. They are hungrier for it, because frankly, they are more starved of it. In just a single phrase, it says convincingly, I believe in you, you can reach for the stars! Applying these techniques is so imperative to disrupting systemic patterns that one more study is worth reinforcing as further evidence to motivate children to persevere.

Like Rosenthal's Pygmalion effect mentioned previously, this shows that the response from teachers who perceived students as higher performers were decidedly different from those that were considered average to low. Imagine how this affects disadvantaged students. When teacher expectations are higher, students perform better. The kinds of implicit biases that cause most unintending adults to miss the mark on this creep up around every corner. If we are not made consciously aware of how our feedback can have such an impact on student success, we reinforce these institutionalized barriers.

The Rosenthal study shows that a teacher's positive expectations influence successful performance. Here again, we can flip the script to support learners in positive and productive ways, by strategizing with higher, more motivational expectations for all learners.

Educators can be implicitly and actively conscientious of this impact and biases that creep into everyday practices. Being aware is half the battle. The rest of ones responsibility is actively and consciously offering students effective solutions that result in their determination to heighten expectations of themselves. The next section will present techniques to accomplish this.

Deep Work Drives Focus and Fulfillment

Deep work is a cognitive practice that includes academic and professional functioning executed with a distraction-free mindset. This stimulates intellectual capacity at its upper limit. In other words, a deep work mindset is the opposite of the highly distracted, anxious, and primal state associated with negative online interactions. Deep work is the theme of Cal Newport's (2022) text by the same name. He outlines high-capacity output performed by a person, or group engaged in deep focus and strengthens this argument with scientific evidence, providing a framework for implementation and a myriad of benefits for engaging in it.

Deep work is highly satisfying, because of the strong sense of fulfillment associated with it. Brain activity is calibrated, and this mental tuning is quite therapeutic for wellbeing. Strip away distractions and impulses and the person enters a higher state; something researchers call a flow state. Flow triggers high theta brain wave activity, considered a sweet spot in the mind to practice a heightened state of wellness.

Achieving a theta state is highly desirable because theta waves channel a brain frequency range related to alertness, attention, orientation, working memory and the enhancement of cognitive and perceptual performances (Jirakittayakorn & Wongsawat, 2017). In other words, high engagement and deep satisfaction.

The benefits of deep work are not just short-term; they last far beyond the completion of a task, or fulfillment of a goal. Gains are linked to long-term personal well-being, life fulfillment and overall contentment. Work performance is characterized as productive and motivational (Robb, 2019). Therefore, employing deep work is not just a short-term fix; it becomes a sustainable solution and lifelong skill that provokes the development of longer term self-regulation skills in students.

As a highly productive and fulfilling way to achieve tasks, deep work offers a healthy dose to respond to negative feelings and experiences. Enlisting an approach that enables an individual to point toward a mindset that increases their qualitative and quantitative function in operative learning and production addresses the performance achievement aspect schools are accountable to. This then aids children in their learning path, a twofold benefit.

Yet for disadvantaged children, a secondary outcome is added as a substantial bonus. Teaching children to engage in and trigger their deep work focus is not only a helpful approach in school, but its impact goes far beyond, offering the lifelong advantages highlighted previously. It benefits learners in tremendous, and substantially longer lasting outcomes.

Deep work results in such vast influence on wellness that it shapes our attitudes in a more positive and constructive manner. Since having a negativity bias is human nature, altering this with a disproportionately higher output of satisfaction and productivity can override that bias by focusing intensely on something that is highly rewarding. It is an invaluable remedy to rewire our brains toward accomplishment with deep satisfaction and serenity, rather than not feeling good enough This lack of self-confidence is one of the most destructive limitations on children, especially disadvantaged learners.

This deep sense of satisfaction is a highly desirable state for learners to aspire to, as they return to experience it again and again. Such a yearning builds on prior accomplishments.

Teaching students to activate a deep focus mindset at will is so beneficial that an exploration of ways to get there is worth teaching students so they can see how to achieve this level of output. Using a variety of techniques is prudent because different methods affect diverse individuals in a variety of ways.

Since different students will master a deep state in their own ways, and one size does not fit all, offering one silver bullet, miracle solution is sure to cause many to fail, much of the time, causing regression rather than progress. Change that trajectory by offering a menu of options, something Gaskell (2021) refers to as stacking, increasing the likelihood of positively influencing a greater proportion of students with multiple methods running across each other.

Accept that while we also increase this probability, getting all students on board is unlikely. Focus on the majority, on patterns of growth, and not perfection in your quest to aid disadvantaged learners. Getting many more kids there is better than few, or none.

Students who face additional challenges gain from tools that enable them to reduce the odds that stubbornly persist against them. Arming children with a set of tools to deploy, on call and when needed, enhances their opportunity to succeed, from within. That is empowering for children who benefit tremendously from this kind of resourcefulness.

Following are a sampling of strategies; this is not an exhaustive list, rather it is a guide for retrieving a variety of options. Since deep work is so satisfying, the self-regulation strategies introduced can directly compete with screen time and other impulses in our distracted world. Helping students gain this state of wellbeing is worth the time and resources to allocate for methods to access it.

Strategies for Eliciting Deep Work in Students

One way to help develop a deep work mindset is by introducing tonal sounds at just the right frequency level to optimally tune one's mind. This has the effect of priming other senses, effectively pulling a person away from unproductive disruptions. This may sound like science fiction hogwash, but read on for the proof and value in employing this strategy.

Coffeehouse Sounds

Teachers can allow students to tune into targeted sounds, and escape into their own safe mental space, while working independently. There are many variations that serve to benefit from this sound effect and an easily accessible one is coffeehouse chatter; sounds that mirror your local coffee shop. Share websites designed to maximize the benefit of this sound as you work, such as coffee house sound resources (Coffitivity, n.d.). Many are easily accessible online, found in abundance at places like YouTube. Using headphones, these sources effectively simulate the background noise level and sound to induce an ideal state of concentration.

Using tonal sound resources like this primes the brain to a surprisingly increased state of focus. By putting a set of headphones on and engaging in focused work while listening to these targeted background noises, a student can achieve strong levels of theta wave processing, focus and productivity.

Does it really work? Why and how can this benefit learners? When students tune into the chatter and clatter of a methodical, busy coffee house, it arouses their mind to center on an ideal sweet spot; a sort of "distracted focus." That is, there is enough indistinguishable ambient noise in the background to offset primal distractors, while allowing higher senses to be ordered, and trained on work.

This chatter offers just enough background noise to pull students away from external stimuli like social media pings and pongs, while facilitating a sensation that arouses them to settle into an ideal focal point. It is compelling to consider that being slightly distracted enables our brains to be more creative, invigorating a resilience to prioritize on important learning tasks.

Binaural Beats—Similar Impact, Different Approach

Binaural beats enable the brain to elicit an interpretation of sound converted for better processing. It works because when two tones are presented to a person, each at a different frequency in separate ears, the brain generates an additional, third perceived tone. This third tone is called a binaural beat. You hear it at the frequency difference between the two tones.

This presents a rhythmic beat to the recipient. Neurons throughout the brain activate electrical messages at the same rate as the perceived beat. Scientists have learned to harness this to create a physiological change within the brain to evoke a response. This response can be tailored in a variety of ways, depending on the brain waves triggered. Some induce a restful, calm state. Others create a deeply focused state, like the ones desired for learners. Still others create a highly energized state, helpful when preparing for exercise, a game or workout.

Getting There

When binaural beats are continuously broadcast into either ear over a period of time, they harmonize with your brain waves. Binaural beats can subsequently change your brain wave pattern, and this can actually change your mindset. So how long does it take, and is it worth the time to invest in a classroom lesson, to encourage a deep state of work and focus?

Research suggests that only three to seven minutes is required to induce the effect that allows your brain to sync up with the auditory stimuli (Jirakittayakorn & Wongsawat, 2017; Yugay, 2021). In a busy classroom with important work to accomplish, teachers should consider: are efforts to provoke engagement of students worth three to seven minutes? Another way to frame this is, in a 40-minute lesson period, is it valuable to gain 33 to 37 minutes of full engagement? The answer should be obvious when the alternative may be zero or far below this range in quantity and quality of engagement.

Given the technology tools that are available to most, including high rates of computer-to-student ratios and cell phone or tablet access, making use of technology to engineer higher states of learning is quite appealing. Using these tools is highly recommended for this reason alone. Employing tools like binaural beats, and other options to make use of sound to help students enter a state of high concentration and deep work should be part of every teacher's toolbox.

Introducing Physiological Responses for Focus and Wellness

A physiological response for priming the brain to navigate away from anxious states, and toward achievement of higher, more focused states of mind serve as an additional resource for teachers. Even better is when a technique requires no additional resources or capital. They are so accessible and inexpensive that we can bring them with us anywhere.

Breathing techniques are conducive to triggering brain patterns to address the anxiety many students face. One option is the 4–7–8 method. When we breathe deeply and systematically, stretch receptors around the diaphragm linked to the parasympathetic nervous system are activated. With the 4–7–8 method a pause in the middle of the 3-step exercise for 7 seconds in the slightly stretched position produces a stronger rest-and-digest effect. This causes an almost massage-like reaction to the diaphragm, a tranquil physiological response.

Visually following this pattern of breathing is essential for learners needing a quick, minutes-long fix. Once practice becomes customary, learning can apply this strategy, at sites that show the learner the expansion and shrinking (*4–7–8 Calm Breathing Exercise—Relaxing Breath Technique | Hands-On Meditation*, 2020) process affecting their body.

Once the student gets acclimated to the practice, they may no longer need the added video or audio to rely on. They become self-regulatory in their management and that provides them with independently managed anxiety reduction. After all, self-regulation for lifelong independence and success is the ultimate goal.

Summary

Radical Principals seize on the moment, stepping into opportunities, bringing a trusting community along with them, and forging a new era where all are given the opportunity to succeed. Punishment is disproportionate to children of color and for those that are disadvantaged in other ways. Yet suspension affects everyone, including non-disciplined children and this has to be addressed for all. Evidence reveals that longer discipline cycles result in exponentially greater negative consequences on a student's future academic performance, attendance, and behavior.

Schools have very little leverage to try new or untested practices. New non-punitive alternatives are often met with resistance by many in the school community. Working around bureaucracy is one of the chief ways to change longstanding practices that harm disadvantaged children. Embracing a series of unconventional methods in a form of bundling, compounding, or stacking interventions and ideas is what builds momentum, not any one silver bullet.

A series of compounding, composite menu options available in the Radical Principals' arsenal are the agents of true and sustaining change. There are three primary ways for radical leaders to forge this path of success and equity for all:

1. Professional Development
2. Leading by example (implementing programs)
3. Teaching students' self-regulation strategies to propel them beyond their disadvantage

Run Edcamp-style faculty meetings for truly purposeful teacher professional growth. Gain consensus that improving instruction, classroom management, student performance and family relations are the umbrella under which we serve virtually all subcomponents for teaching and learning that teachers can gain valued professional development in. Enlist faculty to share best practices, which provide an additive effect to gain from the PD experience.

Using the power of story, radical leaders can help teachers embrace methods for reinforcing equity and putting a stopgap on institutionalizing inequality. When we share stories with children, they can align their thoughts to those experiences and challenges. A powerful technique to employ is sharing stories of our personal vulnerability to show we had to overcome our own challenges.

Helping students achieve deep states of focus and production are highly satisfying ways for them to begin to build on their own momentum, self-regulate and turn the tide against their inevitable circumstances. Implementing tonal sound effects from sources like simulated coffeehouse sounds and binaural beats to engineer a focus by the brain has performance benefits that cannot be shrugged off. Physiological mapping through controlling breathing also functions to assist learners in reducing anxiety.

9

Bringing It All Together

Altering the trajectory of a disadvantaged child's path is one of the most radical and extraordinary opportunities school leaders can embark on. Provided the circumstances that foster opportunity for a child, any student can flourish. Subsequently, their path, appearing slight on the surface, can so profoundly impact that child's direction over time. What if we could strategically modify this trajectory? Let us consider this from the context of charting a course, in small and incremental ways on an upward curve, and in similarly tiny yet increasingly downward declining ways.

When Europeans first charted their course to settle in the New World, navigators discovered that the slightest alteration in course could have profound effects. This is because a few degrees of error may seem small, and it is, for a short trip. Lengthening that trip over thousands of miles, a ship veers so sharply off course, that recovering from this direction is overwhelming, costing time and resources to redirect back on route.

Another example involves charting calculations during space travel. The Apollo missions over the last half-century showed

DOI: 10.4324/9781003275718-9

how necessary it was to be precise. Being off by a few degrees could mean missing the Moon's lunar orbit entirely. This mattered when a broken ship had to be navigated back home. The accuracy could have life and death consequences. Any slight mistake in calculation would have cost the astronauts the chance to sling shot off the orbital surface of the Moon and make their way safely back home.

Back on Earth, the same is true when missing a turn, or walking down the wrong trail on an individual journey. We quickly become misdirected and lost. It does not take long before we are backtracking, having lost unanticipated time and energy. Similarly, the direction of a child's path in life can have large effects with small, subtle shifts.

All children start out on a lifelong journey at birth and, almost instantaneously, some are pointed to a downward trajectory beyond their control, spiraling unjustly in the wrong direction, because of their life circumstances,. Others are nourished with opportunity. The equity gap starts long before children enter the schoolhouse door.

Therefore, blaming schools and the institutionalized inequities that exist as the barriers between children is not only unjust, but also misses the point, being too limited in scope. There are broader social implications within society. While schools can do little to change these conditions, they can serve as grassroots incubators that begin to build a new, opportunistic path for children equipped with equity guardrails.

Let us examine the power of influencing the course in a child's life to point them into the right direction.

One Child's Path

Nile high-fived his teacher. He had just achieved the skills of a new reading level. This milestone included mastery of applying more difficult, abstract concepts, such as inferring from text. He was ready to move onto the next level (synthesizing text) and this step was celebrated by everyone in his classroom community who applauded and encouraged him. While this was one micro moment, and students move through dozens of these landmarks over time, celebrating this micro-win mattered in monumental ways.

Nile was working through a level of literacy his peers had surpassed years earlier. Yet due to his circumstances, he had been racing to catch up ever since. His first language was not English, so he had to accelerate his gains to close the gap. Pausing to enjoy small milestones along the way can have a remarkable effect on Nile's confidence, resilience, and motivation to persevere in a host of ways that does not appear immediately obvious.

Small wins (Gaskell, 2021) are successive tiny milestones of achievement that build on previous achievements, consolidating incremental successes that expand and speed up over time. In corporate America, and capital workplaces, it is common to encourage a route toward long-term success through small wins. Yet little has been documented in research about how small wins benefit students, and especially for our most disadvantaged children.

Students like Nile, who urgently need the most enriching resources to support them, continue to face some of the most substantial obstacles to catch up. How do we begin to offset this immediate and systemic set of disadvantages? Nile needs a method for monitoring his own small wins. This can be accomplished through deliberate measurement techniques that build on collecting and promoting his milestones as a strongly linked and closely tracked incentive. This can be so convincing that it motivates him to persevere beyond challenges that surface along his path. That is where real progress takes place.

Educators have a responsibility to seize on opportunities such as small wins, presenting a shift away from downward declines, to build on a competitive edge that closes gaps. Strategically arranging these for students to proactively strengthen their progress, gradually, through a series of repeated incremental successions and accomplishments begins to produce a cascade of progress.

Build on Small Wins with Gamified Learning and Assessment

Consider introducing small wins from a classroom practice context. Teachers have access to a large inventory of online gamification tools, including well-known programs like Kahoot, Peardeck, and Nearpod. These and other web tools like them allow for assessment of student responses, in quick, targeted bursts. They can be tailored to present visible individual progress markers so learners can see and experience concrete micro victories. Learners are motivated by simply monitoring their own progress markers, encouraged by each consecutive step toward growth.

This is possible because individuals benefit greatly from experiencing forward motion in these continuous, tiny and steady changes. The indicators are subtle, not so far away that the goal seems overwhelming, and unreachable, inaccessible and increasing anxiety. Instead, steady progress markers are just beyond their comfort zone, still close enough that they can be reassured that taking the calculated risk will not overwhelm them.

Looking at this from a set of steps—a handful of these seem reachable, manageable. Dozens of flights that twist and turn, curving endlessly like a bad dream that are unseen, wrapped high and around, looks and feels unknown, inaccessible, and even scary. It is beyond the scope of a learner's capacity to reach for and visualize.

Steven Kotler (2014) considers the optimal range for a task to be just challenging enough to extend the learner slightly beyond their current skill set, motivating them to pursue another step, and then perhaps another. This is a single-digit goal (Lakhiani, 2018); small gains of perhaps 4% that become 8%, which then become 16% and so on. Expanding on these slighter, incremental ranges is not only possible; it also feels extremely productive and encouraging in tangible and quantifiable ways for the learner.

Teachers can track a child's growth in ways that are less stressful, using gamification (Gaskell, 2021). This is the application of common ways to play games (point scoring, competition with others, rules of play) to learn, as an interactive, online technique. It can stimulate a learner's growth through high engagement and motivation. This enables the teacher to monitor a child's progress, measure data points, and establish milestones, collaboratively with the student.

This form of tracking student performance feels desirable for children and helps them visualize their progress, like a growth chart, moving in an imperfect, yet remarkably upward curve. No great success happens in a single straight line and teaching children this helps them realize in invaluable ways. Effective learning naturally occurs this way. Sharing these personalized advances with students helps them to move further (Lenz, 2017) to establish a new learned pattern of resilience.

Brain synapses fire in new patterns, allowing the student to realize different possibilities that they would not have otherwise seen or known existed before. This allows learners and school communities to embark on the grassroots efforts of leveling the playing field, forging a new path of opportunity filled with equality, a model to build from.

This may sound feasible and simple, and it is. That is the power of an approach that builds on micro shifts in the right direction. It is apparent, and conclusive. Students like Nile engage in their own path forward, enabling them to become active participants in their individual learning and development. They realize and are motivated by their progress. Data presented toward their upward trajectory inspires the most uncertain children. See Appendix D for more information on data gamification collection processes.

Where gaps persist and widen, teachers can use methods like these, in a series that reverses the trend and benefits all students to close those equity gaps (Wood, 2020a).

Educators have a tremendous opportunity to close the equity gap, if they approach student learning in their shared experience, and implement these approaches in their classrooms. They can provide bridges that remove injustices. Children like Nile will have the opportunity to help them close gaps with others, to build on their developmental path, stripping away the limitations that unfairly obstruct someone because of who they are. Instead, we allow him to become the very best version of himself, tailored to his unique journey forward *because* of who he is.

Social Media Affects at Risk Populations Far More Dramatically than Others

Radical Principals recognize the prevailing issues that destructive online behavior causes, both in their school, and more broadly across the community. Acknowledging this is one step; considering how to resolve the problem to help students learn more from the problems social media causes is the next step.

This can be a daunting task. After all, aren't the problems of social media beyond our control, and scope as educators? Even if they weren't, how would we even begin to address them? Larger social issues compound these challenges. Yet schools are places where learning opportunities can be a remedy to these problems. Educators can help children most in need learn how to skillfully benefit, rather than be harmed by online engagement.

Disadvantaged students are more greatly impacted by the effects of social media, than their peers who experience more support, protection, and opportunities to be shielded from harmful outside effects. This may sound counterintuitive to reality. After all, don't wealthier, advantaged children have more access and free time, and therefore are more inclined to be exposed to the negative effects of screen time?

Evidence points in the opposite direction. Disadvantaged children are more vulnerable to the negative effects of screen time, further deepening the equity divide between them and their peers, rather than leveling it.

Problematic behaviors include underlying characteristics that many children involved in negative social media experience, increasing their vulnerability. These include factors that can compound screen time issues. Attention deficit hyperactivity disorder (ADHD), social anxiety, and depression are a few. A greater proportion of disadvantaged groups face these, resulting from traumatizing experiences, and the impact of trauma can be multiplied by the ill effects of being online.

The reason? "Teens are really driven by their peers," motivated by peer interactions, Dr. Radovic explains. "They're exploring their identity, being creative, and sharing things that they've done, but it's difficult for them to filter out the negative" (Klass, 2021). These filtering mechanisms become even more difficult to access when students are already at risk. Next, is an exploration of why some of the most popular online tools endanger our most susceptible learners more significantly.

Instagram is a common communication platform used by millions of children every day. Instagram's owner Facebook revealed knowledge about the negative effects of mental health its platform poses on children, especially girls. Whatever the reasoning for knowing and not addressing these concerns, this came to light through fact-finding and whistle-blower campaigns. This attention reinforced what was widely believed to be a concern among psychologists, neuroscientists, researchers, and educators.

While the attention highlighted female students, boys are negatively impacted too. One in seven boys in the United States (i.e. millions) reported that Instagram made them feel worse about themselves (Wells et al., 2021). That prevalence was evidenced by a broad spectrum of respondents. This number is almost certainly higher for at-risk and disadvantaged populations. Additionally, daily screen time exposure is increasing, further subjecting students to potentially negative online experiences.

Children typically spend four hours a day onscreen. This number grew much higher during the Covid-19 pandemic. In the United States alone, screen time doubled, to nearly eight hours per day. This may suggest the natural effect of so many students being sheltered away in seclusion. Certainly, this was one way out, an instrument of connection for many to bridge the gap that caused such unimaginable isolation, triggering many to replace social opportunities in person by reengaging digitally with friends and loved ones.

This connection served a useful purpose in many scenarios. Healthy online alternatives will be presented later in the chapter. Yet unfortunately, the alarming result was often the contrary, with destructive impacts on children. Adolescents engaging in social media and video chat often did not have the benefit of fostering social connection. Rather, it was found that teens felt less social support during the pandemic (Nagata, 2021), even with online communication mechanisms available to them. Some of this was due to a lack of awareness about online support and education resources.

Worse, the children in greatest need of more healthy supports experienced the least amount of care: While screen time increased for all respondents, Black teens, Hispanic teens and those from lower-income households demonstrated evidence that they spent more time on screens than the general population (Nagata, 2021). Since most children did not suddenly become more resourceful in where or how they engaged, it is probable these groups had less information on access to beneficial care.

Why? Nagata (2021) explains this likely resulted from a lack of financial resources for alternative activities and less access to safe, outdoor spaces. Even during a pandemic, individuals with resources could find other outlets to engage peers or family members and were able to have more information available to them about productive online alternatives.

Traveling to safe open spaces and meeting others in person were some of the ways individuals with access and support could escape to safer spaces and experiences. Additionally, simply knowing the option existed is liberating, as opposed to the confinement that individuals with less resources encountered.

The value of accessing outdoor spaces, and in nature were addressed in Chapter 4, and there is convincing evidence of its connection to wellness, intelligence and health for individuals who learn about and enjoy the benefits associated with being outside. When there is less access for students, we must be prepared to offer and teach them about the alternatives.

There is abundant evidence to reinforce the broad concern that social media has harmful effects on students. Since it has been established that this is even more pronounced in individuals facing greater obstacles, be encouraged to know that there are solutions.

The Antidote to a Distracted and Stressful Online World

We cannot easily limit student access to digital experiences. Furthermore, inhibition does not preclude desire. Even if schools and families were to shield children from the damaging effects of social media, how would this prepare them to deal with online challenges in the future, when they gain greater independence? How would they learn to face newfound exposure, absent the familiarity or preparation we can offer them?

Indeed, social media and the technological resources children have access to are so tightly woven into the fabric of their daily routine and activities that expecting them to relinquish access, or to be guided faultlessly through its use are both impractical expectations. Instead, educators, families and communities should practice how best to navigate being online. We must point children in the right direction when they engage in their day-to-day interactions.

The greatest asset is for learners to become so adept at regulating healthy online alternatives that they can learn to leverage it, rather than suffer from it. Schools can embrace the responsibility, as arbiters of learning, to support children and their families in this important developmental milestone of their online experience and presence.

Strategies to counter the negative effects of social media are presented as ways to address the distractibility that comes from digital interference. This helps all individuals be more present and avoid constant interruptions from screen time. It also demonstrates for students that being offline in social settings can be a fulfilling experience, with the many benefits associated with it, as mentioned in Chapter 4.

This can help students academically, too. Consider one study, which revealed that one half of the students were engaged in online interactions instead of class instruction (Hazelrigg, 2019). Clearly, these students were less productive, less likely to learn or retain any content and utterly disengaged. Short of being in class, they gained little value from being present.

One of the most damaging effects of distracting online behavior, especially during learning and interactions, is when it pulls the person away from opportunities for higher-level thinking, as highlighted earlier. Our senses are driven toward primal urges when engaging in dopamine-inducing online urges.

This lowers our desire to gain, or regain focus. Adding to this effect, we are not paying attention to the rewarding learning opportunities offered when replacing them with primal hits from online feedback loops. Following are proposed strategies to fight the effects; methods that are time tested and researched, and aid all students, especially the most disadvantaged.

Solutions

One way to alter the effects of online disruptions is to help those impacted to become consciously aware by demonstrating concrete effects. Taking the time to prove for families and students the impact of social media is an important step—awareness can begin the process. By portraying the many examples of negative consequences from being online, we can emphasize the value to recognize potential costs. One way to accomplish this is through teaching about something called the *disinhibition effect*. This has destructive costs and providing alternative choices to replace the effect can positively influence students.

Disinhibition effect is the perception that an individual assumes they are obscured, anonymous; can act freely, and separately from oneself. Therefore, acting out in ways that they would not normally appears to carry minimal to no consequence. This has the effect of creating a negative, risky cycle of interactions that result in damaging implications on the individual, and others. This is because they believe they can turn this conduct on or off as quickly as a light switch. They are wrong.

One way to help students realize these interactions are real and consequential is to engage in discussions with them about how the online disinhibition effect separates their authentic self from this far harsher online version. This has the effect of spelling out the reality that they can easily jeopardize themselves when shifting their behavior for the worse, entering a dangerous zone of online misconduct.

Being unaware of the impact often plays a large part in the role of destructive behavior. This leads to more damaging behaviors that spiral, in both the short and long run. Perceiving anonymity online can propel this contrast. Showing students that they are not anonymous, and that this unhealthy behavior does not serve to benefit them further helps to establish self-awareness. It helps to deter them from behaving more harshly than their authentic self ever would.

Another educational opportunity for treating and teaching about the online disinhibition effect is to distinguish between the harmful effects of this dilemma, and how to leverage it for one's own advantage.

There is even a contrast for this. It is called the *benign disinhibition effect*. This is quite literally the opposite of the disinhibition effect. The benign disinhibition effect results from the interactions people gain from feeling safer when expressing themself online rather than in person. This is due to their being able to use privacy to serve as a protective layer of safe support in groups that are actively monitored to insure both good conduct and personal privacy.

The benign disinhibition effect has shown that individuals can produce a willingness to seek out help and for them to open up to others who are not part of their offline life. When positive support is objectively substituted online, individuals can experience a significant effect on the incentive of their first-person words (Lapidot-Lefler, 2015). This enables the person to feel heard, empathized with and supported by others, in a less judgmental way than when someone intimately and personally knows them. The safety of anonymity works in their favor.

Helping students understand that they can have access to appropriate safe spaces online for their own positively nurturing sustenance is an alternative therapeutic way out for those who might otherwise feel trapped. This offers the option to replace negative consequences of online social media with positive ones. By teaching children to differentiate between positive and negative access points online, they can learn how to self-regulate when they go online on their own.

One of the greatest challenges in helping learners manage social media behavior and their presence online is connected to the breakdown in motivation toward the pursuit of a goal. Frequent social media use is linked to memory deficits, especially in the person's transactive memory—the kind of thought processes that filter what information is important enough to store in the brain and what information should be discarded (Fotuhi, 2020).

Losing focus and concentration are the biggest costs resulting from on-screen distractions. Restoring these is a valuable tool in the management of any self-aware child. Having brought about a level of consciousness, children can use what once were the sources of their distraction to regain attention. Employing tools to steer individuals toward attention and creativity presents a compelling advantage for countering the effects of social media disruptions, especially when redirecting to more functional and fuller engagement.

Teach Students to Differentiate Between False Narratives and Real-life Images

While tapping self-regulation mechanisms helps students to train their minds on learning priorities and away from the primal distractions of social media, another factor is the age-old peer pressure associated with peer groups. Children are often caught up in unhealthy comparison webs, tricked into believing a fictional narrative played out on social media.

Concretely demonstrating to students that their peers and role models do not have idealistic lives is a powerful way to deter the risk of a student's mental health being jeopardized. Encouraging learners with evidence that illustrates this can and must be presented to help them decipher reality and feel liberated from many of the unhealthy pressures associated with online comparison.

A study of three groups of women viewing "Instagram vs reality" images (Tiggemann & Anderberg, 2019) demonstrated that viewing real images, and distinguishing these from fictional, idealistic versions of others, resulted in increased body satisfaction for those seeing the real difference, relative to the ideal images. The harmful effects of appearance comparison were far much less for the "reality" image group than for an "ideal" image control group. That is, providing students a healthy dose of reality about appearance is a tremendously beneficial way for them to see how versions of other people are exaggerated or false, and that they can indeed measure up.

Consciously teaching students that online, enhanced images are unrealistic and not based in reality can help them detach from fictional portrayals. They can instead constructively attend to and enjoy authentic versions, while feeling good about them-selves. This is a valuable tool to institute because it offers an outlet for students who may otherwise feel stuck by systems of self-judgment that pressure them during impressionable and highly vulnerable phases of their life.

Discouraging Costly Behaviors

More than two-thirds of American students enroll in post-sec-ondary institutions after graduating (Vlasova, 2021), making their process for acceptance into a program a competitive phase in most late teens' lives. Many of the remaining students seek skilled trades and professions, which require training as they aspire for job security and higher wages. What can be damaging to students seeking a secure future are the impulsive decisions they make online before they even embark on their post gradu-ate opportunities.

Teaching students that their online behavior is far more conse-quential and not nearly as anonymous as they might assume, and that their misconduct can be incredibly costly if they act unethi-cally, is another way to help them understand the consequences of on-screen activity. This helps curb bad online behavior. The fact that penalties can result may serve as a deterrent to inhibit their bad online behavior. This is especially relevant during a time in life when students have not fully developed cognitively, therefore allowing them to make logical long-term decisions under pressure.

Soley implementing a fear-based approach in isolation is not enough. Like any compliance-based method, it only lasts if indi-viduals fear repercussions, in the short term. It does not provide for practical long-term solutions. Children commonly question authority, even when it is obvious that this approach bears a negative reaction. Applying this deterrent as part of a larger sys-tem of interventions is more logical. To reiterate, interventions are more impactful when stacked together, rather than serving as standalone solutions by themselves.

Since social media behavior can cause negative consequences on both the mental wellbeing and future livelihood of students, this has an even greater significance on already disadvantaged children lives. Good practices, such as teaching students about the personal significance of online conduct and strategies to redirect toward deep work should be employed for all. Disadvantaged populations must be prioritized, with sustained support in order to impact change.

Educators must repeatedly reinforce that students are not nearly as anonymous as they may believe they are while engaging in online conduct. Smith et al. (2021) explains how colleges can easily locate students' social media posts and interactions. In fact, 25% of college admissions offices specifically employ research methods to investigate their entrant's online conduct. The percentage of colleges checking online will continue to increase.

These factors play a significant role in practices post-secondary institutions and employers institute for vetting students as candidates. Also consider institutions who may unintentionally discover student misconduct when it is active and averse online. Students should come to understand that they are not anonymous online, and educators can take advantage of opportunities to impress this on them. Provide specific examples to illustrate the reality of this active and ongoing monitoring process.

One example of repercussions for online misconduct took place when ten students had met rigorous Ivy League standards. They were admitted to a prestigious school, Harvard University, only to have their admissions status revoked, after the university learned that they had posted obscene commentary online.

Consider the difficulty of entering an Ivy League tier school, only to have that destroyed because of a few poor decisions online, never mind the challenges of finding a new school, with other institutions blackballing red-flagged students. Being aware of such newsworthy incidents like these highly publicized portrayals pose unnecessary barriers for students

There Are Solutions

An intriguing Australian study examined student social media behavior before, during and after receiving direct instructional guidance on the consequences of online misconduct. The researchers found that instituting a proactive instructional approach helped students develop significantly longer-term reductions in anonymity perceptions and toxic online disinhibition (Barlett et al., 2020) effects.

Combining a coordinated multi-tier system to teach students better online engagement holds promise for students, especially those with less access to other opportunities. Consider the following series of approaches when implementing a practical approach to help learners in need:

1. Educate students about the repercussions of bad online behavior. Show specific examples such as the Harvard case, as an incentive for avoiding bad online conduct.

   —*Do this: Use strategies like teaching about the Australian study, by providing video and/or article reviews for demonstration and discussion of how no one can hide behind anonymity when misbehaving online.* Review the overall impact of mental wellness.

2. The Instagram reality versus fantasy study is a concrete illustration for learners to decipher fictional online narratives from reality.

   —*Do this: Review the Instagram study with learners and ask them to perform a role play that mirrors the experience under the safe supervision of school officials.*

3. Offer alternative strategies to engage in more focused, less disruptive, and unhealthy behaviors, such as distracted focus techniques.

> —Do this: While students are working on a task independently in class, have them place their phone out of arm's reach (and screen side turned over), Plug headphones into their computer and play coffeehouse background sounds at a website like Coffitivity (cited earlier): Having facilitated this, you can encourage learners to incorporate tonal focus sounds into their routine when at home, while working on homework, researching or any independent task that requires high levels of concentration.

Offering a combined approach is likely to yield a far more effective outcome than any one of these strategies operating alone. This is not meant to minimize the value of any one of them. Rather, it is to point out that when you compound with a multifaceted approach, the results are likely to become more coordinated, synergized, consolidated, effective and, therefore, yield farther-reaching outcomes.

Responding to the harmful effects of misguided online conduct, especially for children in the greatest need of support, is a significant factor in the Radical Principal's toolkit. Acting proactively to boldly get out in front of the challenges is not only a good idea, but it should be considered obligatory, not just a consideration. Seeing this issue as too big to bite off is not acceptable, when children most in need are affected. Breaking interventions into small achievable sets as outlined helps mitigate this large social dilemma that affects children in need.

Radical action must be taken, and particularly when introducing step-by-step processes. These serve as a guide, a roadmap. If you find other ideas to combine with these, or to substitute with, remember that your context is different than anywhere else, so try it. What works is what matters. Address your unique circumstances with the best tools you have access to. The suggested practices outlined offer a sound starting point. It is the concept of combining feasible interventions for your school that are most important to apply.

Summary

Small shifts equal major adjustments, long term. Embracing this ideology allows school leaders to help guide students and the faculty teaching them to manage outcomes that produce big dividends, especially for disadvantaged children. Small wins foster massive payouts and understanding this psychology arms students, especially those who need it most to be successful, breaking beyond institutional barriers.

Using tools like gamification can help teachers track, monitor and celebrate the progress of their students. It also helps students to experience micro wins in ways that motivate them to aspire toward greater and greater success.

Social media can have incredibly destructive impacts on students, especially those most in need. Teaching children how impactful their online conduct is can help both their mental wellbeing, and their future. Consequences can set in motion unalterable paths that create even more disadvantages, creating a cycle for those struggling. Helping students find alternatives both on- and offline in place of unhealthy and unproductive online behaviors has incredibly positive benefits.

Finding safety valves, like the benign disinhibition effect, can aid learners in their own wellness and management of self. Safe alternatives for dangerous online areas will support learners in ways that go beyond and help them to self-regulate their own behaviors, in impactful ways. Learning to differentiate fictional narratives, as in the Instagram versus reality study, are healthy lessons for students to engage in. Consequences are too weighty for learners to subject themselves to due to poor online decision-making and impulses.

Reversing this trajectory is most effective through stacking by teaching learners the consequences of bad online conduct, exposing learners to reality versus perceived highlights. Steering students toward more productive, deep focus methods for aiding learners is far more beneficial in the long run. Offering a combined approach is likely to yield a greater effective result than any one of these approaches, as a standalone.

Remember that your context is different than anywhere else, so try it. What works is what matters.

Appendix A

Breakdown of Time lost due to lateness to class

Eight 42-minute periods daily = 336 minutes' total instructional time.

2.5 minutes lost per six instructional passing times =15 minutes per day.

15 minutes lost per day = 1 lost class every third day. One lost day every 24 days.

This totals on a 180-day calendar, 7.5 days of instruction time lost, forever!

Appendix B

List of positive behavior intervention resources, both mine and those I have adopted and adapted…

Implementing the Positive to Negative Ratio in Schools (Gottman)

John Gottman discovered that the singular differential between happy and unhappy couples was the balance between positive and negative interactions during conflict. A specific ratio makes for lasting relationships.

The ratio is a minimum of three positives to 1 negative interactions.

"When the masters of marriage are talking about something important," Dr. Gottman says, "they may be arguing, but they are also laughing and teasing and there are signs of affection because they have made emotional connections."

Unsuccessful relationships demonstrate far fewer positive interactions to compensate for their increasing negativity. If the positive-to-negative ratio drops lower than the 3–5:1 range, the likelihood of failure in the relationship is so high, it often results in divorce.

Applying the Elements of Praise

Whitaker (2020) referred to features of successful teachers and determined praise was a critical characteristic. He referenced five fundamentals of effective praise when delivering praise to students (Whitaker, 2020).

(a) authentic—recognizing authentic acts or accomplishments
(b) specific—should relate to something recognizable to the student that warranted the praise
(c) immediate—given in a timely manner
(d) clean—not contingent on reciprocity and not delivered to neutralize criticisms
(e) private—many students prefer praise separate from others to avoid resentment from other students or perceived as a teacher's favorite

===

Check In/Check Out A system engaging of students in daily checking in with an adult at the start of school to review daily goals and provide encouragement. Teachers document feedback to monitor the student's day. Students check out at the end of the day with a teacher, and the student is prepared for nightly preparation and organization returning the following morning to check in.

(https://www.pbisworld.com/tier-2/check-in-check-out-cico/)

Hall Races (Gaskell, 2020)—incentives are awarded to the first hallways cleared, creating a positively competitive spirit that prompts students in groups of classes to work together to "win." Decreases discipline and increases time on task.

Middles to Littles (Gaskell, 2021)—a strategy to incentivize at-risk or troubled adolescents, especially those with literacy delays to read to preschool students. The program redirects positive attention to students accustomed to negative attention and has been shown to reverse the discipline cycle, while adding to a school climate and culture.

Mentoring—get faculty and staff who do not have students in their class connected (eliminates grade bias). Finding ways to make this works results in the following for children in need:

Young Adults Who Were At-Risk for Falling Off Track but Had a Mentor Are:

55% more likely to enroll in college

78% more likely to volunteer regularly

90% are interested in becoming a mentor

130% more likely to hold leadership positions (greater than 100% because they can hold multiple leadership positions)

Source: https://www.beamentornow.org/why-mentoring

Schoolhouse Adjustments (Gaskell, 2021)—integrates retired police officers who serve as school security with students who come from disadvantaged backgrounds to build bonds and provide a secondary mentoring source that helps everyone see this relationship through a different lens—culture-shifting as well as reinforcing for positive school climate.

Behavior Observation Chart (Gaskell, 2021) is another tracking tool. It establishes a baseline of undesirable behavior that is charted out over time, and then a goal is set for a reduction in undesirable behavior. This is agreed upon with the student and replaces desired behavior. Observed behaviors are tracked with students' knowledge and encouragement, and reward are earned by the child as something they select from a menu (example 5 minutes on a game Fridays).

Appendix C

EdCamp-style faculty meetings:

1. **Designate an organizer**.
   Anyone can be the organizer: a principal, supervisor, teacher leader, or even a respected informal leader in your school. Basically, you need someone with faculty-wide influence.
2. **Create a topic list**.
   Survey your faculty on the topics they are interested in learning about. You can do this using Google Forms or informally, especially if you have direct access to faculty suggestions.
   Next, build a list of ideas, with choices to allow faculty to select from a menu.
3. **Develop a registration process**.
   Set up a Google Form to allow faculty to sign up for their choices. Google Forms allows you to limit the number of choices.
4. **Schedule room locations**.
   Once the number of sessions and assigned faculty has been established, assign rooms, close together to minimize transition time between. Use a mail merge tool to access faculty selections from the spreadsheet associated with the form they submitted and create a personalized invitation to each session. This personalized invitation makes it feel welcoming and helps organize the event.

5. **Emphasize to faculty that this is an opportunity to stimulate their interest**.
Edcamp-style faculty meetings are adaptable, so faculty can experiment as a group to troubleshoot together. Edcamps also offer faculty the opportunity to share ideas about how they might use a newly learned concept.

6. **Consider this as a continuum**.
After an Edcamp meeting, encourage ongoing learning and reinforcement There are three important ways to reinforce and celebrate the learning:

♦ Issue personalized certificates of completion. You can find templates easily online.

♦ Follow up with survey feedback (what went well, what suggestions do they have, what would they like to see at a future session).

♦ Offer follow-up PD in team, department, or future faculty meetings, based on their needs/requests.

Appendix D

Gamification Resources for student success:

Kahoot is among the most popular games and has a procedure to collect data from performance responses. In Kahoot, teachers can download responses to a spreadsheet, and determine the frequency of incorrectly answered prompts. This enables the teacher to quickly diagnose patterns of problems, both within a whole class and by student, allowing for targeted teaching to a group or an individual.

Nearpod offers a presentation-style method for engaging students in interactive activities, which prompt them for responses that are collected. As in Kahoot, teachers can identify a class-wide summary of correctly answered prompts, and errors. Additionally, individual student responses can be identified and downloaded as a spreadsheet or PDF for selected supports.

Peardeck operates like Nearpod, serving as a teacher presentation tool that prompts collectible student responses. Student responses download easily to a spreadsheet, where they can be evaluated for performance, patterns and more. Peardeck is a broader presentation resource, where accessibility of student data provides critical capture points to gain knowledge about students' understanding of lesson material. It is excellent for a social studies, science, or language arts lesson.

Flipgrid offers an intuitive audiovisual collection device that works well for archiving student video responses in a digital portfolio format to track their performance over time. For example, the user-friendly interface allows for archiving portfolio-style video to help a world language or English teacher measure literacy development.

Padlet and other online sticky-note-style forums also provide downloadable information about students. Teachers can use Padlet to gather learner responses to track over time as a story or learning concept develops.

Bibliography

4–7–8 Calm Breathing Exercise – Relaxing Breath Technique | Hands-On Meditation. (2020, January 15). [Video]. YouTube. https://www.youtube.com/watch?v=1Dv-ldGLnlY

Allday, R. A., & Pakurar, K. (2007). *NCBI. Journal of Applied Behavior Analysis*. Retrieved December 27, 2021, from https://www.ncbi.nlm.nih.gov/pmc/articles/PMC1885415/

Álvarez, B. (2021, September 10). *School suspensions do more harm than good | NEA. National Education Association*. Retrieved November 28, 2021, from https://www.nea.org/advocating-for-change/new-from-nea/school-suspensions-do-more-harm-good

Ballard, E. S. (2002). *Three letters from Teddy. Catholic Education Resource Center (CERC)*. Retrieved January 17, 2022, from https://www.catholiceducation.org/en/faith-and-character/faith-and-character/three-letters-from-teddy.html

Barlett, C. P., Heath, J. B., Madison, C. S., DeWitt, C. C., & Kirkpatrick, S. M. (2020). You're not anonymous online: The development and validation of a new cyberbullying intervention curriculum. *Psychology of Popular Media*, 9(2), 135–144. https://doi.org/10.1037/ppm0000226

Bridges, W. (2022). *Transitions [Deluxe Edition] 2nd (second) edition Text Only* (2nd ed.). Lifelong Books.

Byrne, J. E. M. (2017, September 13). Time of day differences in neural reward functioning in healthy young men. *Journal of Neuroscience*. Retrieved December 5, 2021, from https://www.jneurosci.org/content/37/37/8895

Coffitivity. (n.d.). *Coffitivity*. Retrieved April 14, 2022, from https://coffitivity.com/

Collinger, T. (2016, January 4). *Northwestern Now*. Retrieved April 13, 2022, from https://news.northwestern.edu/stories/2016/01/opinion-techcrunch-reviews

Coyle, D. (2013, December 13). *The simple phrase that increases effort 40%. Daniel Coyle.* Retrieved November 29, 2021, from http://danielcoyle.com/2013/12/13/the-simple-phrase-that-increases-effort-40/

Effective Principal 360°. (2009). *Berkleyleadership.Com.* Retrieved July 13, 2022, from https://www.berkeyleadership.com/pdf/Principal%27s%20Observer%20Assessment.pdf

Eitner, J. (2019, August 8). *Keyboard warriors and social media muscles in schools. BAM! Radio Network.* Retrieved July 9, 2022, from https://www.bamradionetwork.com/keyboard-warriors-and-social-media-muscles-in-schools/

Epperson, A. (2019, May 9). *How much do school suspensions really hurt? PBIS Rewards.* Retrieved December 11, 2021, from https://www.pbisrewards.com/blog/how-much-do-school-suspensions-really-hurt/

Foster, E., & Wiseman, L. (2014, February 13). *ASCD express 9.10 – A multiplier environment. ASCD Express.* Retrieved January 2, 2022, from http://www1.ascd.org/ascd-express/vol9/910-foster.aspx

Fotuhi, M. (2020, December 11). *What social media does to your brain. NeuroGrow.* Retrieved from https://neurogrow.com/what-social-media-does-to-your-brain/

Gainsbury, S. M., Browne, M., & Rockloff, M. (2019, June 1). Identifying risky Internet use: Associating negative online experience with specific online behaviours. *SAGE Journals.* Retrieved November 5, 2021, from https://journals.sagepub.com/doi/full/10.1177/1461444818815442

Gambini, B. (2018, September 26). *Your Facebook friends don't mean it, but they're likely hurting you daily. University at Buffalo.* Retrieved December 30, 2021, from http://www.buffalo.edu/news/releases/2018/09/034.html

Gaskell, M. (2018, December 13). *Looking for a way to lower suspensions and reduce bullying? eSchool News.* Retrieved April 12, 2022, from https://www.eschoolnews.com/2018/12/10/looking-for-a-way-to-lower-suspensions-and-reduce-bullying/2/

Gaskell, M. S. (2020). *Microstrategy magic* (1st ed.). Rowman & Littlefield.

Gaskell, M. S. (2021). *Leading schools through trauma* (1st ed.). Routledge.

Grant, A. (2021). *Think again: The power of knowing what you don't know.* Viking.

Greenemeier, L. (2018, March 8). *You can't handle the truth – At least on Twitter. Scientific American.* Retrieved December 18, 2021, from https://www.scientificamerican.com/article/you-cant-handle-the-truth-at-least-on-twitter/

Hampton, S. (2021, April 20). *MCTE middle school teacher of the year acceptance speech. Writing Mindset.* https://www.writingmindset.org/blog/2019/10/19/mcte-middle-school-teacher-of-the-year-acceptance-speech?format=amp

Hazelrigg, N. (2019, July 10). *Survey shows nearly half of students distracted by technology. Inside Higher Ed.* https://www.insidehighered.com/digital-learning/article/2019/07/10/survey-shows-nearly-half-students-distracted-technology

Jirakittayakorn, N., & Wongsawat, Y. (2017, June 28). Brain responses to a 6-Hz binaural beat: Effects on general theta rhythm and frontal midline theta activity. *Frontiers in Neuroscience.* Retrieved from https://www.frontiersin.org/articles/10.3389/fnins.2017.00365/full

Johnson, S. S. (2021). Addressing mental health and substance use disorders amid and beyond the COVID-19 pandemic. *American Journal of Health Promotion, 35*(2), 299–301. https://doi.org/10.1177/0890117120983982a

Kahneman, D. (2012). *Thinking, fast and slow.* Penguin.

Kaiser, R. B. (2020, March 2). *The best leaders are versatile ones. Harvard Business Review.* Retrieved December 12, 2021, from https://hbr.org/2020/03/the-best-leaders-are-versatile-ones

Kamenetz, A. (2018, December 17). *NPR. National Public Radio.* Retrieved November 28, 2021, from https://choice.npr.org/index.html?origin=https://www.npr.org/2018/12/17/677508707/suspensions-are-down-in-u-s-schools-but-large-racial-gaps-remain

Klass, P., MD. (2021, September 23). *When social media is really problematic for adolescents. The New York Times.* Retrieved November 4, 2021, from https://www.nytimes.com/2019/06/03/well/family/when-social-media-is-really-problematic-for-adolescents.html

Lapidot-Lefler, N. (2015, July 1). The benign online disinhibition effect: Could situational factors induce self-disclosure and prosocial behaviors? | Lapidot-Lefler | Cyberpsychology: Journal of

Psychosocial Research on Cyberspace. *Journal of Psychosocial Research on Cyberspace.* Retrieved November 4, 2021, from https://cyberpsychology.eu/article/view/4335/3402

Nagata, J. M., MD. (2021, November 1). *Screen time use among US adolescents during the COVID-19 pandemic: Findings from the adolescent brain. Jama Network.* Retrieved November 4, 2021, from https://jamanetwork.com/journals/jamapediatrics/fullarticle/2785686

Newport, C. (2022). *Deep work: Rules for focused success in a distracted world [Paperback] [Jan 01, 2016] Newport, Cal.* Little, Brown Book Group.

Nocera, J. R., Mammino, K., Kommula, Y., Wharton, W., Crosson, B., & McGregor, K. M. (2020, December 6). *NCBI – WWW error blocked diagnostic.* U.S. National Library of Medicine National Institute of Health. Retrieved December 26, 2021, from https://www.ncbi.nlm.nih.gov/pmc/articles/PMC6950538/

Oregon Student Dress Codes. (2016, January 5). [Video]. YouTube. https://www.youtube.com/watch?v=r7G7KXDI4vI&feature=youtu.be

Parker, I. (2012, January 30). *The story of a suicide. The New Yorker.* Retrieved April 11, 2022, from https://www.newyorker.com/magazine/2012/02/06/the-story-of-a-suicide

PBSIS. (n.d.). *Rutgers Robert Wood Johnson Medical School.* Retrieved December 27, 2021, from https://rwjms.rutgers.edu/boggscenter/projects/pbsis.html

Phelamei, S. (2019, November 7). *What happens to your body when you look at your phone first thing in the morning? Times Now.* Retrieved December 26, 2021, from https://www.timesnownews.com/health/article/what-happens-to-your-body-when-you-look-at-your-phone-first-thing-in-the-morning/512627

Pink, D. H. (2019). *When: The scientific secrets of perfect timing* (Reprint ed.). Riverhead Books.

Poets.org – Academy of American Poets. (n.d.). *If – Academy of American Poets.* Retrieved March 25, 2022, from https://poets.org/poem/if

Portell, M. (Host). (2021, November 14). Michael Gaskell – Trauma informed educators network podcast (No. 52) [Audio podcast episode]. In Trauma Informed Educators Network Podcast. Soundcloud. https://soundcloud.com/mathew-portell-93233744/episode-52-michael-gaskell-trauma-informed-educators-network-podcast?utm_ campaign=social_sharing&utm_source=mobi&utm_terms=mobi_display_ads_experiment.low_floor_price

Robb, A. (2019, February 5). *The 'flow state': Where creative work thrives. BBC Worklife.* https://www.bbc.com/worklife/article/20190204-how-to-find-your-flow-state-to-be-peak-creative

Ropeik, D. (2018, March 8). *School shootings are extraordinarily rare. Why is fear of them driving policy? Washington Post.* Retrieved December 18, 2021, from https://www.washingtonpost.com/outlook/school-shootings-are-extraordinarily-rare-why-is-fear-of-them-driving-policy/2018/03/08/f4ead9f2-2247-11e8-94da-ebf9d112159c_story.html

Rosenthal, R, & Jacobsen, L. (1968). *Pygmalion in the classroom: Teacher expectation and pupils' intellectual development.* Holt, Rinehart and Winston.

Schwerdt, M. (n.d.). *Mrs. Jones, Winner of the NH Catholic School teacher of the year award. Saint Francis School.* Retrieved November 2, 2021, from https://www.stfrancisschoolnh.org/mrs-jones-winner-of-the-nh-catholic-school-teacher-of-the-year

Shukla, A. (2021, January 13). *Online disinhibition effect: Why we express more online. Cognition Today.* Retrieved April 16, 2022, from https://cognitiontoday.com/online-disinhibition-effect/

Smith, R., Abdukadirov, A., & Smith, R. (2021, June 25). *Can colleges see your Snapchat, Instagram, TikTok? – College reality check. College Reality Check.* https://collegerealitycheck.com/can-colleges-see-social-media/#:%7E:text=Up%20to%2025%25%20of%20college,of%20recommendation%2C%20and%20admission%20essay.

Soto, S. (2018, May 25). *Attention all type a teachers: We need to chill out. Medium.* Retrieved December 12, 2021, from https://medium.com/@teamteachon/attention-all-type-a-teachers-we-need-to-chill-out-769552ce883c

Thompson, A. (2021, February 5). *Meditation vs. Sleep: What's the difference? MindMojo.* Retrieved December 31, 2021, from https://www.mindmojo.co/journal/2017/7/24/meditation-vs-sleep

Tiggemann, M., & Anderberg, I. (2019, November 19). *SAGE Journals: Your gateway to world-class research journals. SAGE Journals.* Retrieved November 5, 2021, from https://journals.sagepub.com/doi/full/10.1177/1461444819888720

Vlasova, H. (2021, May 9). *What percent of high school graduates go to college? (2021). Admissonly.Com.* Retrieved November 5, 2021, from https://admissionsly.com/percentage-who-go-to-college/

Weir, K. (2020, April 1). *Nurtured by nature Psychological research is advancing our understanding of how time in nature can improve our mental health and sharpen our cognition. American Psychological Association.* Retrieved January 4, 2022, from https://www.apa.org/monitor/2020/04/nurtured-nature

Wells, G., Horwitz, J., & Seetharaman, D. (2021, September 14). *Facebook knows Instagram is toxic for teen girls, company documents show. WSJ.* Retrieved November 4, 2021, from https://www.wsj.com/articles/facebook-knows-instagram-is-toxic-for-teen-girls-company-documents-show-11631620739

Werner, E. E., & Smith, R. S. (2001). *Journeys from childhood to midlife: Risk, resilience and recovery.* Cornell University Press.

Wessling, S. B. (2014, April 18). *A secret to great teaching: Maintain a beginner's mindset. Teaching Channel.* Retrieved February 15, 2022, from https://www.teachingchannel.com/blog/beginners-mindset

West-Rosenthal, L. B. (2020, January 16). *5 branding basics for school leaders. We Are Teachers.* Retrieved February 26, 2022, from https://www.weareteachers.com/how-to-define-your-school-brand/

Whitaker, T. (2020). *What great teachers do differently* (3rd ed.). Eye on Education.

Whitaker, T., Pollak, S. R., & Echo Point Books & Media, LLC. (2020). *Shifting the monkey: The art of protecting good people from liars, criers, and other slackers.* Echo Point Books & Media, LLC.

Wood, J. (2013). *Organisational behaviour: Core concepts and applications* (3rd ed.). John Wiley and Sons Australia.

Wood, S. (2020a, October 8). *CCRC playbook provides recommendations to address equity gaps in dual enrollment programs. Diverse: Issues in Higher Education.* Retrieved January 4, 2022, from https://www.diverseeducation.com/institutions/community-colleges/article/15107912/ccrc-playbook-provides-recommendations-to-address-equity-gaps-in-dual-enrollment-programs

Wood, W. (2020b). *Good habits, bad habits: The science of making positive changes that stick* (Reprint ed.). Picador.

Yugay, I. (2021, November 9). *How to use binaural beats to get the most benefits. Mindvalley Blog.* Retrieved December 4, 2021, from https://blog.mindvalley.com/how-to-use-binaural-beats/

Zill, N., & Wilcox, B. (2019, November 19). *The black-white divide in suspensions: What is the role of family? Institute for Family Studies.* Retrieved November 28, 2021, from https://ifstudies.org/blog/the-black-white-divide-in-suspensions-what-is-the-role-of-family

For Product Safety Concerns and Information please contact our EU
representative GPSR@taylorandfrancis.com
Taylor & Francis Verlag GmbH, Kaufingerstraße 24, 80331 München, Germany

www.ingramcontent.com/pod-product-compliance
Ingram Content Group UK Ltd.
Pitfield, Milton Keynes, MK11 3LW, UK
UKHW021433080625
459435UK00011B/250